Study Abroad and Early Career

Higher Education Policy Series 35
ERASMUS Monograph No. 21

Study Abroad and Early Career

Experiences of Former ERASMUS Students

Friedhelm Maiworm and Ulrich Teichler

Jessica Kingsley Publishers
London and Bristol, Pennsylvania

The right of Friedhelm Maiworm and Ulrich Teichler to be identified as authors
of this work has been asserted by them in accordance with the Copyright,
Designs and Patents Act 1988.

First published in the United Kingdom in 1996 by
Jessica Kingsley Publishers Ltd
116 Pentonville Road
London N1 9JB, England
and
1900 Frost Road, Suite 101
Bristol, PA 19007, U S A

Library of Congress Cataloging in Publication Data
A CIP catalogue record for this book is available
from the Library of Congress

British Library Cataloguing in Publication Data
Maiworm, Friedhelm
Study abroad and early career : experiences of former
ERASMUS students. - (Higher education policy ; 35)
1. Foreign Study 2.Employment in foreign countries
3. Vocational guidance
I. Title II. Teichler, Ulrich
370.1'96

ISBN 1-85302-378-7

Printed and Bound in Great Britain by
Cromwell Press, Melksham, Wiltshire

Contents

Preface

The European Community Action Scheme for the Mobility of University Students (ERASMUS) was established by the Council Decision of 15 June 1987. The Programme is open to all types of higher education institution and all subject areas, and aims to promote wide-ranging institutional cooperation for activities related to teaching. As of 14 March 1995, it became one part of the new EU programme in the field of education, SOCRATES, which offers opportunities for cooperation for every area of educational provision, with the aim of thereby improving the quality of European education at all levels. SOCRATES comprises ERASMUS, COMENIUS (for school-level education), LINGUA (promotion of language learning), Open and Distance Learning, Adult Education, plus various activities concerned with the exchange of information and experience

ERASMUS supports a number of different activities, broadly divided into 'mobility' actions (for students and staff) and 'curricular' actions (including the development of new courses, intensive programmes and measures to ease cross-border recognition through use of the European Credit Transfer System or ECTS), the latter extending the benefits of European cooperation to a wider audience than those able to take advantage of a mobility programme. Under SOCRATES, ERASMUS activities have evolved to take account of the changing environment as well as feedback from participants over the years. Two new developments deserve particular mention: one is the move to increase the institutional support given to European cooperation activities through the introduction of a so-called 'institutional contract', and the other is the encouragement, through Thematic Network Projects, to academics to examine the future directions for university studies in Europe. The student mobility part of the programme has been, and remains, however, a very important part of ERASMUS.

As ERASMUS takes on its new role under the SOCRATES programme, it is important to remember that the impact of a study period abroad can extend well beyond the academic year in which it takes place, and can affect many more lives than merely those directly involved. This study, looking at the longer lasting effects of student mobility from the point of view of the students themselves, complements the series of regular surveys of student experiences undertaken over the period of the programme. Knowing the likely impact not only provides valuable information to those responsible for running the ERASMUS programme, whether at European, national or local level; it also helps the wider public to appreciate the position of ERASMUS relative to the more general context of life in Europe today.

Interesting studies on ERASMUS form part of the ERASMUS Monograph series. The series listing appears elsewhere in the current volume. The information contained in the present study does not necessarily reflect either the position or the views of the European Commission.

Chapter 1

Aims and Methods of the Study

The European Community Action Scheme for the Mobility of University Students (ERASMUS) established in 1987 has provided for large numbers of students to study for a few months or a whole academic year at a European partner institution of their home institution of higher education. This type of student mobility is aimed to broaden students' academic and cultural experience through mobility within Europe. If such a study period is successful, we might expect it to have an impact not only on the remaining period of study, but also beyond the study period, i.e. the transition to work as well as at least the early career and work tasks.

This study is based on a third questionnaire survey responded to by students and former students who had spent a period of study in another member state of the European Community during the academic year 1988/89, i.e. the second year of the ERASMUS programme, supported by a supplementary fellowship provided by the European Community.

(1) In winter 1989/90, 3,212 students having studied during the preceding academic year in another member state of the European Community replied to the questionnaire "Experiences of ERASMUS Students 1988/89" (see the publication of the findings in F. Maiworm, W. Steube and U. Teichler. *Learning in Europe: The ERASMUS Experience*. London: Jessica Kingsley Publishers, 1991).

(2) In spring 1992, i.e. almost three years on average after return from the study period abroad, those former ERASMUS students who had responded to the first questionnaire and had provided an address were mailed a second questionnaire "Experiences of 1988/89 ERASMUS students five years after returning from their study period abroad". 1,339 former ERASMUS students actually responded (see the publication of the findings in U. Teichler and F. Maiworm. *Transition to Work: The Experience of Former ERASMUS Students*. London: Jessica Kingsley Publishers, 1994).

(3) In spring 1994, i.e. about two years later, thus almost five years after return from the study period in another member state of the Euro-

pean Union, the former ERASMUS students were sent the third questionnaire "Experiences of 1988/89 ERASMUS Students Five Years After Returning from Their Study Period Abroad" and 1,234 persons responded. About five years after the return from the study period abroad, former ERASMUS students could be expected to have completed their study and could be asked to provide information on a broad range of topics concerning their early career and professional activities:

- major activities since the second survey,
- completion and possible prolongation of study,
- development of employment and early career,
- current professional activities,
- foreign language competence and knowledge about the host country,
- the role international competences play in search and recruitment as well as in the work assignments during the early career stages,
- maintaining of contacts and skills,
- assessment of impacts of the study period abroad.

Table 1.1
Return Rate, by Country of Home Institution of Higher Education

Country of Home institution	Valid addresses		Respondents		Return rate
	Number	Per cent	Number	Per cent	
B	150	6.8	76	6.2	50.7
D	493	22.4	349	28.3	70.8
DK	18	0.8	11	0.9	61.1
E	263	11.9	129	10.5	49.0
F	455	20.7	258	20.9	56.5
G	32	1.5	14	1.1	43.8
I	237	10.8	128	10.4	54.0
IRL	33	1.5	19	1.5	57.6
NL	102	4.6	46	3.7	45.1
P	8	0.4	3	0.2	37.5
UK	411	18.7	201	16.3	48.9
Total	2,202	100.0	1,234	100.0	56.0

B = Belgium	F = France	NL = The Netherlands
D = Germany	G = Greece	P = Portugal
DK = Denmark	I = Italy	UK = United Kingdom
E = Spain	IRL = Ireland	

The third questionnaire was mailed in February 1994. Responses received by July 1994 are included in the subsequent analysis. It was mailed, like the second one, to those 2,573 persons of the 3,212 respondents to the first questionnaire who had provided their address. A reminder letter was sent in April 1994 to former ERASMUS students who had not returned the questionnaires within eight weeks. Actually, 371 questionnaires were returned, because the addresses had become invalid in the meantime and the mail could not be forwarded. It is appropriate to assume that far more addresses had become invalid but that not all of these questionnaires were returned because of different mailing rules and practices in the European countries. Altogether, 1,234 former ERASMUS students responded to the third questionnaire. The response rate was 56 per cent. It varied by country of home institution from 38 to 71 per cent, as Table 1.1 shows.

The first questionnaire was responded to by about 67 per cent of about 4,800 former ERASMUS students for whom their coordinators had originally provided addresses. The second questionnaire was responded to by about 28 per cent and the third questionnaire by about 26 per cent of those initially addressed. The so-called "panel mortality" was lower than one usually expects in the framework of longitudinal studies. Notably, the loss at the third stage was relatively small, because questionnaires were also sent to those who did not respond to the second questionnaire. Actually, 30 per cent of those responding to the third questionnaire had not responded to the second one.

However, among those responding to the third questionnaire, the number of former students from some countries and some fields of study was too small to allow valid statistical analysis. Eventually, fewer than 10 respondents each responded who initially studied in Portugal, who spent the ERASMUS-supported period in Denmark, and who had studied communication sciences. In those cases, figures, though presented in the tables, will not be consistently mentioned in the text.

Formal checks of the responses and the coding of open questions were taken care of by members of the research team with the help of students from the respective countries. The data processing and statistical analysis was undertaken on the UNIX computer of the Comprehensive University of Kassel and on IBM personal computers at the Centre for Research on Higher Education and Work. Programme packages SPSS5.0 served the statistical analysis and the provision of tables.

The three surveys of this longitudinal study are part of a programme of surveys, statistical analyses and other studies undertaken by the Centre for Research on Higher Education and Work (Wissenschaftliches Zentrum für Berufs- und Hochschulforschung) of the Comprehensive University of

Kassel (Universität Gesamthochschule Kassel) in Germany. The studies supported by the Commission of the European Communities aim to monitor and to evaluate the ERASMUS programme on the basis of information provided by key actors and recipients of support. In addition to the students (both those mobile in the framework of Inter-University Cooperation Programmes and in the framework of the European Community Course Credit Transfer System), the coordinators of Inter-University Cooperation Programmes, the local directors, those in charge of supporting the ERASMUS programme in the administration and finally those teaching for some period in another European country in the framework of ERASMUS teaching staff exchange were asked to state their experiences. A synthesis of the findings of all the studies undertaken in this framework will be completed in 1996.

The study was eased by substantial support from the ERASMUS Bureau and the European Commission. Formal checks of the responses and the coding of open questions were performed by Angela Antona, Skarlatos Antoniadis, Klaus Klein, Bernhard Krede, Isabelle Le Mouillour and Sabine Stange. Word processing was undertaken by Paul Greim and Kristin Gagelmann.

Chapter 2

The ERASMUS Programme

2.1 Context and Aims

Most experts agree in assuming that international competences – defined widely in an operational manner, i.e. competences enriched by knowledge and experience typically not or to a lesser extent fostered by institutions of a single nation – will become more and more important for coping with new academic challenges and with changing job requirements in a growing number of highly qualified occupations. We note trends of globalization, internationalization and Europeanization in the world of knowledge and scholarship as well as the world of work which are confronted with a persistence of national focus or of national characteristics of teaching and learning in higher education and are not easily replaced or complemented by boundary-crossing perspectives.

Study abroad might be a means of acquiring a new mix of competences suitable to meet these new challenges and demands. For even if the mainstream of curricula and other study provisions serves other purposes, the mobile students would be a flexible element serving the necessary change. He or she might select or might be provided in a targeted manner with knowledge essential for the desired nature of competences.

The European Union, founded during the 1950s under a more specific name for purposes of economic cooperation in select areas, started to promote student mobility on an experimental basis in 1976 in the framework of the so-called Joint Study Programmes (JSP). When the scope of European educational activities broadened in the mid-eighties, ERASMUS (acronym for European Community Action Scheme for the Mobility of University Students) was inaugurated in 1987 as the most visible of the various European educational programmes and as the largest support scheme for student mobility and related cooperation among higher education institutions ever established, in terms of the number of students and institutions involved.

ERASMUS is a financial support scheme of the European Union primarily promoting temporary student mobility within European countries. Large numbers of students are provided with grants aimed at covering the additional costs for a period of study, lasting mostly between three months and one year, in another country of the European Union or another European country included in ERASMUS.

Students are, as a rule, financially supported if they are mobile within networks of departments (or a few pluri-disciplinary networks of institutions). The networks formed for this purpose, called Inter-University Cooperation Programmes (ICPs), may be granted support for part of costs incurred in managing student mobility. They apply both for students' and institutional grants. Only a small number of individually mobile students, so-called "free movers", are awarded support in the framework of ERASMUS.

Specific grants are made available for language training, academic and administrative staff visits, staff mobility for teaching abroad, short intensive programmes, and joint curriculum development. Some of these grants are provided to the ICPs only in the context of institutional support for student mobility, some might be applied for separately and alternatively even might be the prime purpose of the establishment of an ICP, whereas other grants can be applied for individually by academic and administrative staff.

Student and institutional support is provided under the condition that participating departments are likely to recognize upon return the achievements made during the study period abroad as part of and equivalent to study at the home institution. Targets of financial support as well as criteria for selection, additionally, reflect the view that various organized means of supporting student mobility academically and administratively, such as preparatory programmes, provisions for foreign languages learning, help in the search for or provision of accommodation, administrative and academic advice and support for incoming students etc. can serve to offset the risks and efforts involved in settling in and adapting to a foreign higher education environment as well as to living in another country. Also efforts in favour of curricular integration, for example through elements of joint curricula and possibly joint selection of students, mandatory periods abroad, certification of study achievements abroad and possibly even a double degree, are considered as "good practice". Though not explicitly stated as selection criteria for the award, they tend to be viewed as likely to increase the success of temporary study abroad.

It might be added that some other activities are supported in the framework of the ERASMUS programmes which are not the focus of the surveys addressed here. Some departments cooperate in large networks aiming to recognize study abroad by means of a standardized credit transfer system. This so-called ECTS (European Community Course Credit Transfer System) was inaugurated in 1989/89. Further, ERASMUS provides grants for short study visits aiming to establish international cooperation, supports a network of national information centres involved in information of mobile students and possibly recognition of their study achievements. Finally, grants are available for associations, evaluation projects, publications etc. linked to mobility and cooperation in higher education.

2.2 Structural and Quantitative Development

In 1987/88, i.e. the year of inauguration of the ERASMUS programme, about 300 Inter-University Cooperation Programmes were awarded support. In 1988/89, the first full-fledged year of ERASMUS and the year in which the respondents of the survey presented here spent a study period abroad, 895 ICPs were awarded support. The respective figure grew to more than 2,000 ICPs in 1994/95.

The number of partnerships, i.e. the number of departments or in exceptional cases institutions joining a specific ICP, was altogether 823 in the year of inauguration and 2,618 in 1988/89. Subsequently, it grew to about 10,000. The number of higher education institutions involved (in sending and/or receiving students) was 416 in 1987/88 and 631 in 1988/93 and reached about 1,400 in the mid-nineties. While statistically speaking, only about one-sixth of eligible institutions participated in the ERASMUS programme in 1988/89, we actually observe that almost all major widely known institutions and large institutions of higher education were involved in the ERASMUS programme.

In 1988/89, 2.9 departments on average cooperated within a network. Sixty-one per cent of the networks had only two partners, and only 7 per cent had more than five partners. On average, 11 students were mobile within an ICP, whereby a department sent and received on average four to five students. While about half of the participating departments sent and received at most three students, a few departments sent and received dozens of ERASMUS students.

The number of students mobile in the framework of the so-called Inter-University Cooperation Programmes was about 3,000 in 1987/88 and

9,357 in 1988/89, i.e. the year the students went abroad who were addressed in the surveys discussed here. In the mid-nineties, the annual number of ERASMUS students eventually reached about 70,000. It might be added here that the number of students mobile in the framework of ERASMUS tends to be overestimated, because the European Commission tends publish the aggregate of students estimated by the ICPs in their respective applications.

2.3   Profile of the Former ERASMUS Students

For the sake of convenience, former ERASMUS students will be referred to by the country of their home institution of higher education at which they were enrolled prior to the ERASMUS-supported study period abroad. For example, "British", "French" or "Spanish" would mean that the former students' home institutions were in the United Kingdom, France or Spain, respectively. This is because all the major issues of this study refer to contacts or cooperation between partner institutions of higher education from the respective countries. One should bear in mind, though, that 2 per cent of the former ERASMUS students were foreigners, i.e. not citizens of the country of the home institution of higher education, or had a dual citizenship.

The largest proportion of former ERASMUS students responding to the third questionnaire had been enrolled in business studies (34 per cent) during the period abroad, followed by foreign language studies (16 per cent), law (11 per cent) and engineering (10 per cent). Altogether 29 per cent, 1 to 4 per cent each, were represented in the remaining fields of study or groups of fields presented in Table 2.1. Five per cent of former ERASMUS students enrolled in another field of study between return from the study period abroad and graduation than the one in which they were enrolled during the study abroad period. Fifty-one per cent of the respondents were female.

About 56 per cent of the respondents were 21 – 23 years old at the end of their study period abroad. Altogether, only 14 per cent were older than 25 years and the average age reported was 23.3 years. Most French (22.2 years on average) and British students (22.1 years) were relatively young, whereas Danish students (24.5 years) were the eldest on average.

The differences in the age at the time of the study abroad period reflect to some extent – in addition to the age at the time of first enrolment – the timing of the study abroad period in the course of study. Altogether, 24 per cent of the respondents had spent the ERASMUS-supported period abroad during the first two years of study, 31 per cent during the third year, 19 per cent during the fourth year, and 26 per cent at a later stage.

Table 2.1
Major Field of Study During the ERASMUS-Supported Study Period Abroad 1988/89, by Country of Home Institution of Higher Education
(per cent of respondents five years after the ERASMUS study period)

	B	D	DK	E	F	GR	I	IRL	NL	P	UK	Total
				Country of home institution								Total
Agricultural sciences	0	0	0	2	2	7	0	0	9	0	0	1
Architecture, urban and regional planning	7	1	0	1	2	0	16	5	0	0	2	3
Art and design	1	1	0	2	0	0	2	0	4	0	1	1
Business studies, management sciences	17	44	36	19	35	14	26	16	9	67	43	34
Education, teacher training	3	2	0	2	0	7	1	0	2	0	0	1
Engineering, technology	13	16	36	4	15	0	2	11	0	0	5	10
Geography, geology	0	0	0	4	0	7	1	11	0	0	0	1
Humanities	4	4	0	12	1	0	5	5	0	0	3	4
Languages, philological sciences	4	11	0	29	21	0	16	11	17	0	20	16
Law	32	11	0	11	8	36	9	0	28	0	5	11
Mathematics, informatics	5	2	0	6	2	0	5	0	0	0	1	3
Medical sciences	0	2	0	2	0	0	1	0	2	0	1	1
Natural sciences	0	5	0	2	5	14	2	26	9	33	6	5
Social sciences	4	2	18	4	2	0	8	11	9	0	2	3
Communication and information sciences	1	0	0	0	0	14	1	5	2	0	0	1
Other areas of study	9	0	9	2	5	0	8	0	9	0	8	4
Total	100	100	100	100	100	100	100	100	100	100	100	100
(n)	(76)	(349)	(11)	(129)	(258)	(14)	(128)	(19)	(46)	(3)	(201)	(1234)

Questionnaire 1, question 2.3b: Please state your major field of study and tick the respective group of fields during the study period abroad.

On average, respondents spent 7.5 months abroad in the framework of the ERASMUS grant scheme. As Figure 2.1 shows, 34 per cent spent 4 – 6 months, another 37 per cent 7 – 12 months, 22 per cent a shorter period (three months or in a few cases less) and the remainder even more than 12 months abroad (mostly a second year supported by ERASMUS in cases where the respective course programme requires more than one year abroad in more than one other country).

Figure 2.1

Duration of the ERASMUS-Supported Study Period Abroad 1988/89, by Country of Home Institution of Higher Education

(per cent of respondents five years after the ERASMUS study period)

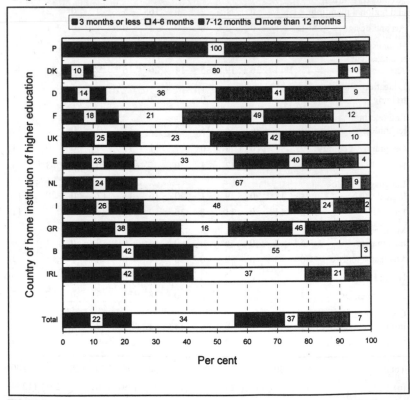

Questionnaire 1, question 2.4: Please state the duration of the ERASMUS-supported period abroad (including work placement and holiday periods).

About 64 per cent of the respondents to the third questionnaire had been solely engaged in full-time study during the ERASMUS-supported study period abroad and a further 11 per cent in part-time study. Twenty-two per cent of students had worked – 19 per cent in addition to study and three per cent solely in that activity. Two per cent had mentioned other study-related activities, such as work on theses. The work placement periods had lasted more than four months on average.

Around 14 per cent reported that both parents were graduates from universities, and in an additional 24 per cent of the cases, only the fathers (21 per cent) or only the mothers (3 per cent) were graduates. The percentage of students with highly educated parents (either one or both of them) varied substantially according to home country, as Table 2.2 shows. It was highest in Belgium (48 per cent), Greece (43 per cent) and Italy (42 per cent), between 30 and 40 per cent in the majority of member states of the European Union, and lowest in Denmark (20 per cent).

Table 2.2
Parents' Higher Education Attainment, by Country of Home Institution of Higher Education (per cent of respondents five years after the ERASMUS-supported study period)

	Country of home institution											Total
	B	D	DK	E	F	GR	I	IRL	NL	P	UK	
Both	17	8	10	13	19	14	19	16	0	33	15	14
Father only	29	23	10	23	14	29	22	16	33	0	17	21
Mother only	1	1	0	3	3	0	2	0	2	0	6	3
None	52	67	80	61	64	57	58	68	64	67	62	63
Total	100	100	100	100	100	100	100	100	100	100	100	100
(n)	(75)	(345)	(10)	(127)	(253)	(14)	(125)	(19)	(42)	(3)	(197)	(1210)

Questionnaire 1, question 1.4: What is the highest level of education attained by your father and mother?

Former ERASMUS students were also asked whether they had been engaged in any other activities besides a general educational career pattern for at least six consecutive months prior to the ERASMUS-supported period. Altogether 25 per cent had been engaged in one or several of those activities. Ten per cent were employed for some period, 9 per cent spent some time in military service, etc.; 7 per cent participated in vocational training, and 5 per cent reported extended travel. On average, former ERASMUS students had spent about 5 months engaged in activities outside the regular educational career patterns prior to the ERASMUS-supported period.

More than 80 per cent had spent some period abroad since they were 15 years old prior to the ERASMUS-supported period, with more than half of them even spending some period in the host country prior to their ERASMUS visit. The average total duration of stays abroad was about six months (for all respondents), of which two months were spent in the ERASMUS host country. Travel abroad varied to some extent by home country. Notably, students from various southern European countries travelled less prior to the study period abroad.

Chapter 3

Graduation and Further Study Activities

3.1 Prolongation of the Total Period of Study

Responses by former ERASMUS students to the first questionnaire, i.e. the survey undertaken a few months after the ERASMUS-supported period, indicated that the overall study period might have been prolonged substantially due to the study period abroad.

Those students who completed their studies within the five year period after the ERASMUS-supported period 1988/89 had initially expected a prolongation of 3.3 months on average. In response to the third questionnaire, they estimated that the total duration of study was actually prolonged by 2.9 months due to the study period abroad. The few respondents who had not completed their study at the time of the third survey initially expected a longer prolongation, i.e. 4.5 months on average. Surveyed five years later, they expected a higher prolongation of 5.4 months on average due to the ERASMUS-supported period.

It is fair to say that students had, on average, a relatively realistic expectation regarding prolongation shortly after the ERASMUS-supported study period abroad. About two-thirds provided identical figures in responses to both the second and third questionnaire, and only in less than a fifth of the cases did the earlier estimate clearly differ from the estimate provided some years after graduation. On average, the prolongation of study attributed to the ERASMUS-supported period about five years after by graduates was one-eighth shorter on average than expected immediately after the ERASMUS-supported period. As Table 3.1 shows, notably British and Greek graduates reported a clearly lesser prolongation than they had expected initially.

Table 3.1

Expected Prolongation* and Real Prolongation** of Study, by Country of Home Institution of Higher Education (mean in months, graduates responding five years after the ERASMUS-supported study period)

	Country of home institution										Total
	B	D	DK	E	F	GR	I	IRL	NL	P	UK	
Expected prolongation	.3	4.2	2.3	2.0	2.5	6.1	3.9	1.0	1.1	6.0	4.6	3.3
Real prolongation	.5	4.2	2.8	1.6	2.4	4.3	3.4	.9	2.2	4.0	2.7	2.9
(n)	(57)	(299)	(10)	(103)	(136)	(10)	(85)	(16)	(34)	(1)	(169)	(920)

Questionnaire 1, question 4.11: The study period abroad is likely to prolong the total duration of my study by:

Questionnaire 3, question 2.2: By how long (if at all) do you believe the study period abroad prolonged the overall duration of your course of study?

* Prolongation of the total study period due to ERASMUS-supported study expected immediately after the ERASMUS-supported period abroad

** Prolongation of the total study period due to ERASMUS-supported study estimated about five years after the ERASMUS-supported period abroad

As Table 3.2 shows, 53 per cent of these former students had not expected any prolongation when asked shortly after the ERASMUS-supported study period. Eleven per cent had expected some prolongation, and 36 per cent assumed that the prolongation of the overall study period would be more or less as long as the whole study period abroad. Five years later, the proportion of those not having really prolonged their study was slightly higher, i.e. 57 per cent.

The prolongation actually estimated five years later corresponds to 41 per cent on average of the study period spent abroad in the framework of the ERASMUS programme. Though slightly smaller than initially assumed, these figures demonstrate noteworthy problems of recognition. The proportion of graduates who reported in the third survey that the prolongation of the overall study period was more or less as long as the whole study period abroad was highest among graduates from Denmark (50 per cent), Italy (48 per cent) and Germany (46 per cent). On the other hand very few Belgian (5 per cent) and less than 20 per cent of graduates from Ireland and Spain prolonged their overall study by the duration of the period abroad.

Table 3.2

Ratio of Prolongation Expected* and Ratio of Real Prolongation** of Study, by Country of Home Institution of Higher Education (per cent of graduates five years after the ERASMUS-supported study period)

	B	D	DK	E	F	GR	I	IRL	NL	P	UK	Total
				Country of home institution								Total
Ratio of prolongation expected												
None	95	32	60	76	74	11	24	75	74	0	55	53
Less than 50%	2	4	0	4	4	11	11	0	9	0	0	4
50 – 74%	0	14	0	1	4	33	5	13	0	100	0	6
75 – 99%	0	1	0	0	0	0	2	0	0	0	0	1
100%	· 4	49	40	19	17	44	57	13	18	0	45	36
Total	100	100	100	100	100	100	100	100	100	100	100	100
(n)	(57)	(269)	(10)	(99)	(117)	(9)	(82)	(16)	(34)	(1)	(158)	(852)
Ratio of real prolongation												
None	91	36	50	78	65	33	33	75	59	0	73	57
Less than 50%	2	3	0	3	5	11	10	0	6	0	0	3
50 – 74%	2	13	0	0	7	22	9	13	3	100	1	7
75 – 99%	0	2	0	1	0	0	1	0	0	0	0	1
100%	5	46	50	18	23	33	48	13	32	0	25	32
Total	100	100	100	100	100	100	100	100	100	100	100	100
(n)	(57)	(269)	(10)	(99)	(117)	(9)	(82)	(16)	(34)	(1)	(158)	(852)

Questionnaire 1, question 4.11: The study period abroad is likely to prolong the total duration of my study by:

Questionnaire 3, question 2.2: By how long (if at all) do you believe the study period abroad prolonged the overall duration of your course of study?

* Prolongation of the total study period due to ERASMUS-supported study expected immediately after the ERASMUS-supported period abroad in per cent of the duration of the ERASMUS-supported period abroad

** Prolongation of the total study period due to ERASMUS-supported study estimated about five years after the ERASMUS-supported period abroad in per cent of the duration of the ERASMUS-supported period abroad

Regarding field of study about half of the graduates from agriculture, communication sciences and education/teacher training prolonged the overall study period by the duration of the whole study period abroad. The respective proportion was lowest among graduates from medical fields (15 per cent).

Of those who perceived some prolongation according to the third survey and named reasons for it,

- 50 per cent argued that they had acquired an additional qualification. By choosing courses abroad which did not match the home curricula, they had to take into account some prolongation.

A larger proportion of those stating reasons for prolongation, however, noted problems which have to be attributed to the cooperating departments and institutions (several respondents named two or more reasons).

- 34 per cent noted a mismatch between courses as a reason for prolongation,
- 33 per cent faced overlapping terms, and
- 29 per cent experienced incomplete recognition by the home institutions.

Finally, the proportion of those noting individual problems was clearly smaller.

- 20 per cent of those prolonging named the reduced workload abroad as the major or as one of the reasons, and
- 13 per cent indicated personal reasons.

3.2 Graduation

Almost all of the former ERASMUS students who had spent a period of study in another member state of the European Community during the academic year 1988/89, reported in spring 1994 that they had been awarded a degree since they had returned (94 per cent). A few former students decided not to complete or failed to complete their studies, and 3 per cent were still studying at the time the third survey was conducted. As Table 3.3 shows, the proportion of those not yet having completed their studies five years after the ERASMUS-supported period was highest among Italian (12 per cent) and Danish students (9 per cent), i.e. students of some of the countries known for frequent prolongation of study.

Table 3.3

Subsequent Award of Degree in Course of Study Enrolled in During the ERASMUS-Supported Study Period Abroad 1988/89, by Country of Home Institution of Higher Education (per cent of respondents five years after the ERASMUS study period)

	Country of home institution											Total
	B	D	DK	E	F	GR	I	IRL	NL	P	UK	
Yes	99	93	91	98	95	100	86	95	91	100	98	94
Not yet	0	5	9	1	1	0	12	5	4	0	1	3
No completion intended	1	1	0	2	5	0	2	0	4	0	1	2
Total	100	100	100	100	100	100	100	100	100	100	100	100
(n)	(76)	(349)	(11)	(129)	(258)	(14)	(128)	(19)	(46)	(3)	(201)	(1234)

Questionnaire 3, question 2.1: Have you subsequently been awarded the degree in the field and course of study in which you were enrolled during your study period abroad 1988/89?

Table 3.4

Overall Duration of Study, by Country of Home Institution of Higher Education (per cent and mean in years, graduates responding five years after the ERASMUS-supported study period)

	Country of home institution											Total
Years	B	D	DK	E	F	GR	I	IRL	NL	P	UK	
2	1	1	0	1	7	9	1	17	0	0	6	3
3	4	0	10	3	22	18	6	17	0	0	9	8
4	19	32	40	9	45	18	29	56	14	0	81	39
5	63	23	20	61	17	36	26	11	24	0	3	25
6	10	30	10	19	6	0	21	0	48	0	2	17
7 and more	1	15	20	8	3	18	18	0	14	100	1	9
Total	100	100	100	100	100	100	100	100	100	100	100	100
(n)	(68)	(322)	(10)	(117)	(212)	(11)	(105)	(18)	(42)	(2)	(193)	(1100)
Mean	4.8	5.2	4.9	5.2	4.0	4.9	5.4	3.6	5.6	7.0	3.9	4.7

Questionnaire 3, question 2.1: Have you subsequently been awarded the degree in the field and course of study in which you were enrolled during your study period abroad 1988/89?

Table 3.5

Location of Graduation, by Country of Home Institution of Higher Education Institution (per cent of graduates responding five years after the ERASMUS-supported study period)

	B	D	DK	E	F	GR	I	IRL	NL	P	UK	Total
				Country of home institution								Total
Home institution prior to the ERAS-MUS-supported study period abroad	71	67	80	63	49	50	63	50	69	100	69	63
Other institution of home country prior to the ERASMUS-supported study period abroad	4	3	0	2	5	0	1	0	0	0	2	3
Home country, institution unspecified	15	13	10	27	18	21	24	44	31	0	25	20
Institution in ERAS-MUS host country	0	4	10	2	17	21	6	6	0	0	1	6
Institution of other country	0	0	0	0	0	0	0	0	0	0	0	0
Double degree of home and host institution	1	13	0	3	10	0	5	0	0	0	3	7
Not identified	9	0	0	3	2	7	1	0	0	0	1	2
Total	100	100	100	100	100	100	100	100	100	100	100	100
(n)	(75)	(326)	(10)	(126)	(244)	(14)	(110)	(18)	(42)	(3)	(196)	(1164)

Questionnaire 3, question 2.1: Have you subsequently been awarded the degree in the field and course of study in which you were enrolled during your study period abroad 1988/89?

The overall period of study of those former ERASMUS students who had graduated in the meantime was 4.7 years on average:

- 3 per cent graduated after two years of study,
- 8 per cent took three years,
- 39 per cent four years,
- 25 per cent five years,
- 17 per cent six years,
- 9 per cent seven and more years.

It should be noted that former ERASMUS students who had gone abroad in the framework of advanced or graduate courses were asked to name the overall study period, i.e. including the period of study up to completion of their first degrees. Thus, the proportions of those studying for five years or more is higher among all responding than among those being awarded a first degree. As Table 3.4 indicates, the shortest average periods of study were reported by Irish (3.6 years), British (3.9 years) and French students (4.0 years). The longest study periods were named by the few Portuguese students surveyed (7.0 years) as well as by the Dutch (5.6 years) and Italian students (5.4 years).

Table 3.6
Location of Graduation, by Duration of the ERASMUS-Supported Study Period Abroad 1988/89 (per cent of graduates responding five years after the ERASMUS study period)

	Duration of study period abroad in months				Total
	3 or less	4 – 6	7 – 12	13 and more	
Home institution prior to the ERASMUS-supported study period abroad	72	67	58	40	63
Other institution of home country prior to the ERASMUS-supported study period abroad	2	3	4	1	3
Home country, institution unspecified	24	21	19	7	20
Institution in ERASMUS host country	1	2	10	18	6
Institution of other country	0	0	0	0	0
Double degree of home and host institution	0	5	8	34	7
Not identified	2	2	1	0	2
Total	100	100	100	100	100
(n)	(251)	(392)	(427)	(88)	(1158)

Questionnaire 3, question 2.1: Have you subsequently been awarded the degree in the field and course of study in which you were enrolled during your study period abroad 1988/89?

A thorough analysis would take into account the number of years required for graduation in the respective countries, the types of higher education institutions, the field of study and possibly specific regulations of the individual course programmes. The respective data on the required duration of study, however, were not available.

Six per cent of the students who had graduated at the time of the third survey stated that they had not graduated in the home country but in the ERASMUS host country (see Table 3.5). A further 7 per cent had been awarded a double degree upon graduation. As Table 3.6 shows, ERASMUS study periods longer than half a year were far more frequently linked to eventual graduation in the host country than periods of half a year or shorter.

3.3   Further Study Activities After Graduation

Of the former ERASMUS students being awarded a degree, 53 per cent subsequently took up further study during the period between graduation and the time the third survey was conducted. The proportion of those transferring to subsequent study and training seems to be extraordinarily high. Based on national surveys available in various countries on the transition to employment and early careers of graduates, we assume that less than 30 per cent of graduates from institutions of higher education in all member states of the European Community will progress to subsequent study and training upon completion of their degree. Information available does not allow us to analyse possible reasons for the frequent participation in further study and training on the part of former ERASMUS students. We might assume first that those deciding to participate in the ERASMUS programme constitute a somewhat select group with more than average educational motivation, second that study experience abroad has stimulated in some cases interest in further study and third, that European competences are conceived to be better utilized in some cases if they are combined with further education and training.

The proportion of former ERASMUS students naming further study as their major or one of their major activities at the time they responded to the third survey was only 7 per cent. Obviously, whereas most respondents had already completed or discontinued their studies at the time the survey was conducted, many of those undertaking further study conceived this not as a major, but rather as an additional activity.

As Table 3.7 shows, 28 per cent of former ERASMUS students transferred to postgraduate study or postgraduate research immediately or soon after graduation, 13 per cent transferred to another form of advanced study or advanced training, 14 per cent reported that they had undertaken vocational training, and finally, 4 per cent had started other first degree programmes.

Table 3.7
Further Study After Completion of Study Course Enrolled in During the ERASMUS-Supported Study Period Abroad 1988/89, by Country of Home Institution of Higher Education (per cent of graduates responding five years after the ERASMUS study period; multiple reply possible)

	Country of home institution											Total
	B	D	DK	E	F	GR	I	IRL	NL	P	UK	
Postgraduate study/research	49	20	0	37	36	57	31	28	12	33	20	28
Advanced study/ training	12	6	10	20	25	7	18	6	7	0	7	13
Other first degree programme	3	5	0	11	3	14	5	0	7	33	0	4
Vocational training	11	16	0	3	7	21	15	0	29	0	27	14
Not ticked	31	59	90	39	39	29	40	67	50	33	48	47
Total	105	105	100	110	110	129	108	100	105	100	102	106
(n)	(75)	(326)	(10)	(126)	(244)	(14)	(110)	(18)	(42)	(3)	(196)	(1164)

Questionnaire 3, question 2.4: If you have completed your studies in the field and courses of study in which you were enrolled during your study period abroad 1988/89, have you subsequently begun further study?

As Table 3.8 shows, the ratio of those undertaking (any kind of) further study among all ERASMUS graduates in the respective field was highest in education/teacher training (85 per cent), law (83 per cent) and humanities (77 per cent). The lowest ratios in this respect could be observed in business studies (34 per cent), engineering (47 per cent) and mathematics (48 per cent).

Table 3.8
Further Study After Completion of Study Course Enrolled in During the ERASMUS-Supported Study Period Abroad 1988/89, by Field of Study During Period Abroad

(percent of graduates responding five years after the ERASMUS study period; multiple reply possible)

| | Field of study | | | | | | | | | | | | | | | | |
---	Agr	Arc	Art	Bus	Edu	Eng	Geo	Hum	Lan	Law	Mat	Med	Nat	Soc	Com	Other	Total
Postgraduate study/research	46	34	40	14	23	25	64	48	26	48	36	36	61	32	17	24	28
Advanced study/training	8	23	20	12	15	16	0	13	17	13	9	21	5	16	0	6	13
Other first degree programme	0	3	0	3	8	5	0	8	9	4	3	7	2	3	17	0	4
Vocational training	15	11	10	8	38	4	9	20	18	34	3	21	4	18	17	25	14
Not ticked	31	43	40	66	15	53	36	23	40	17	52	36	32	39	50	47	47
Total	100	114	110	103	100	103	109	110	109	116	103	121	104	108	100	102	106
(n)	(13)	(35)	(10)	(399)	(13)	(124)	(11)	(40)	(187)	(134)	(33)	(14)	(56)	(38)	(6)	(51)	(1164)

Questionnaire 3, question 2.4: If you have completed your studies in the field and courses of study in which you were enrolled during your study period abroad 1988/89, have you subsequently begun further study?

Agr = Agricultural sciences
Arc = Architecture, urban and regional planning
Art = Art and design
Bus = Business studies, management sciences
Edu = Education, teacher training
Eng = Engineering, technology
Geo = Geography, geology
Hum = Humanities

Lan = Languages, philological sciences
Law = Law
Mat = Mathematics, informatics
Med = Medical sciences
Nat = Natural sciences
Soc = Social sciences
Com = Communication and information sciences

Chapter 4

Employment and Work

4.1 Major Activities After Graduation

As already stated, almost all of the 1988/89 ERASMUS students (94 per cent of those responding to the third questionnaire) were subsequently awarded an academic degree. Most of these subsequently were employed or gathered other experiences in areas outside higher education:
- 80 per cent of the graduates were employed at least for a limited period in a sector related to their subject,
- 8 per cent experienced a period of employment unconnected to their subject or degree,
- 22 per cent experienced unemployment,
- 12 per cent stated military or other public services,
- 2 per cent carried out a traineeship, and
- 14 per cent stated other activities without specification.

Solely further study activities after graduation were reported by 8 per cent of the graduates.

As Table 4.1 shows, periods of unemployment were most often stated by graduates from the Netherlands (43 per cent), Denmark (40 per cent) and France (29 per cent), whereas German graduates reported the fewest experiences of this kind (16 per cent). These differences are only in part due to the composition of subject areas, but primarily reflect the current situation of the labour market in the respective countries.

None of the graduates from medical fields who responded to the survey and only a few from law, education (8 per cent each) and natural sciences (11 per cent) stated that they experienced periods of unemployment. Clearly above average were the respective proportions among graduates in agriculture (58 per cent), humanities (32 per cent) and foreign language studies (30 per cent).[1] The overall periods of unemployment for each

---

1 Former students of communication and information sciences as well as those of geography were not taken into account, because the absolute numbers in the sample were very small.

respective respondent lasted 6.9 months on average. Noteworthy differences in this respect by home country or field of study of the graduates could not be observed.

Table 4.1

Major Activities Other than Further Study After Return from the ERASMUS-Supported Study Period Abroad 1988/89, by Country of Home Institution of Higher Education (per cent of graduates responding five years after the ERASMUS study period; multiple reply possible)

	Country of home institution											Total
	B	D	DK	E	F	GR	I	IRL	NL	P	UK	
Employment related to the subject	90	78	80	81	75	79	81	83	59	67	88	80
Employment unconnected with the subject	7	6	10	5	2	14	6	22	8	0	23	8
Traineeship	1	2	0	1	0	7	0	0	0	0	4	2
Unemployment	24	16	40	18	29	21	22	22	43	0	23	22
Military/other obligatory public services	29	1	0	13	26	21	22	0	11	0	0	12
Other activities	10	13	20	17	9	7	22	6	14	0	18	14
Only study activities stated	3	13	0	9	9	7	4	6	11	33	3	8
Total	165	130	150	142	150	157	156	139	146	100	159	146
(n)	(68)	(325)	(10)	(125)	(236)	(14)	(106)	(18)	(37)	(3)	(196)	(1138)

Questionnaire 2, question 1: Please state your major activities since returning from your ERASMUS-supported period 1988/89.

Questionnaire 3, question 1: Please state your major activities since Jan. 1st 1992.

In the member states of the European Union, military or other obligatory public services are, if required at all, the exclusive domain of male citizens. About one-fifth of male graduates surveyed undertook these kinds of service after graduation. The respective proportion was almost half among French, Belgian and Italian, but only 2 per cent of male former German ERASMUS students, many of whom reported military or public service prior to their higher education. Danish, Portuguese, Irish and

British former ERASMUS students did not carry out military service, either prior to their study programme, or after graduation.

Most of the male (80 per cent) and female (82 per cent) former ERAS-MUS students stated employment as major activity after graduation. Seventy-three per cent were solely employed related to their subject, 2 per cent solely unrelated to their subject and 3 per cent reported both, employment related and unrelated to their field of study. Periods of employment unrelated to the field of study were most common among British (23 per cent) and Irish graduates (22 per cent). Such periods of employment unrelated to the field of study were more frequently experienced by female (12 per cent) than by male graduates (5 per cent). The data do not allow us to infer the extent to which the latter difference is due to difficulties female graduates face on the labour market, or is a result of individual options.

Almost all graduates from art and design and mathematics stated at least a short period of employment related to the field of study. Above average were the respective proportions also among graduates from architecture (91 per cent), engineering (88 per cent), business studies (87 per cent) and medical fields (86 per cent). Graduates from agriculture (50 per cent) and natural sciences were least often employed accordingly (see Table 4.2).

On average, former ERASMUS students had been employed 31 months[2] at the time the third survey was conducted (periods of employment prior to the ERASMUS-supported period 1988/89 were not included). This applies both to female and male former ERASMUS students. Differences in this respect according to home country and field of study were mainly due to timing of graduation and further study activities.

Seventy-six per cent of graduates employed at the time of the third survey, or for at least some period after graduation, solely stated their home country as the location of employment. A further 12 per cent were employed at home and abroad, and 12 per cent were employed solely abroad. Twenty-four per cent, thus, were employed at least for some period abroad – undoubtedly an extraordinarily high proportion, indicating the substantial impact of the ERASMUS programme. This impact was not confined to the ERASMUS host country, where about half of these internationally-mobile graduates spent a period of employment. About a quarter each were employed in other member states of the European Union and in other countries.

---

[2] The calculation includes only graduates who had responded to both tracer studies. Thus data for the whole period after the ERASMUS-supported period abroad are available.

Table 4.2

Major Activities Other than Further Study After Return from the ERASMUS-Supported Study Period Abroad 1988/89, by Field of Study During the ERASMUS-Supported Period Abroad (per cent of graduates responding five years after the ERASMUS study period; multiple reply possible)

	Field of study*																Total
	Agr	Arc	Art	Bus	Edu	Eng	Geo	Hum	Lan	Law	Mat	Med	Nat	Soc	Com	Other	
Employment related to the subject	50	91	100	87	69	88	73	63	79	64	97	86	59	76	83	69	80
Employment unconnected with the subject	8	6	0	7	0	0	9	13	18	5	6	0	7	14	17	16	8
Traineeship	0	0	0	3	0	0	0	0	1	2	0	0	0	0	0	2	2
Unemployment	58	20	20	22	8	19	27	32	30	8	25	0	11	27	50	47	22
Military/other obligatory public services	33	20	0	11	0	20	9	8	5	13	28	7	4	14	17	10	12
Other activities	25	9	10	14	8	13	9	26	15	15	3	7	9	27	0	12	14
Only study activities stated	8	6	0	5	15	4	18	13	5	22	3	0	26	5	0	6	8
Total	183	151	130	149	100	143	145	155	153	129	163	100	117	162	167	163	146
(n)	(12)	(35)	(10)	(391)	(13)	(123)	(11)	(38)	(183)	(130)	(32)	(14)	(54)	(37)	(6)	(49)	(1138)

Questionnaire 2, question 1: Please state your major activities since returning from your ERASMUS-supported period 1988/89.
Questionnaire 3, question 1: Please state your major activities since Jan. 1st 1992.
* Explanation see Table 3.8.

Graduates who had spent their ERASMUS-supported period in Germany stated most often that they were employed in their former host country (24 per cent). Also, a remarkable proportion of those studying in Italy (20 per cent) and France (17 per cent) were employed in their ERASMUS host country. On the other hand, none of those spending the ERASMUS-supported period in Denmark and Greece and few studying in the Netherlands (2 per cent), Ireland (3 per cent) and in Belgium (6 per cent) were subsequently employed there.

4.2 Status of Graduates at the Time of the Third Survey

Eighty-six per cent of those former ERASMUS students who had been awarded a degree were employed at the time of the third survey, i.e. on average almost five years after the ERASMUS-supported period. Seventy-nine per cent were employed full-time; 7 per cent were employed part-time, on average 51 per cent of a regular work-time; 4 per cent reported that they were unemployed; 5 per cent named education and training as their major activity; and 5 per cent stated other major activities. As compared to the second survey, i.e. almost three years after the ERASMUS-supported period, the proportion of employed graduates increased by about 20 per cent.

Actually only 2 per cent were employed and undertook education or training concurrently (see Table 4.3). These were included in the previous paragraph among those employed. About half of them each studied alongside full-time and part-time employment.

As Table 4.4 shows, the highest proportions of full-time employment at the time of the third survey could be observed among graduates from business studies (87 per cent), medical fields (86 per cent) and engineering (84 per cent). In contrast, education and training as major activities were often stated by graduates from geography/geology (27 per cent) and natural sciences (21 per cent).

In contrast to the findings of the second survey no noteworthy difference between women and men regarding status of employment could be observed five years after the ERASMUS-supported period abroad.

Nine per cent of the former ERASMUS who had graduated up to the third survey were self-employed, i.e. 7 per cent more than at the time of the second survey. The proportion was highest among graduates from architecture (34 per cent) and law (20 per cent).

Table 4.3

Status of Graduates at the Time of the Third Survey, by Country of Home Institution of Higher Education (per cent of graduates responding five years after the ERASMUS-supported study period)

	B	D	DK	E	F	GR	I	IRL	NL	P	UK	Total
					Country of home institution							
Full-time employed	85	85	50	65	74	64	65	82	76	67	87	78
Education/training (without employment)	0	3	10	11	7	7	6	6	2	0	3	5
Education/training and full-time employment	3	1	0	0	0	7	2	0	0	33	0	1
Education/training and part-time employment	1	1	0	1	1	7	1	0	0	0	1	1
Part-time employment (without education/training)	7	6	0	9	3	14	11	12	15	0	2	6
Unemployed	0	1	10	6	8	0	4	0	7	0	3	4
Other	4	3	30	8	6	0	11	0	0	0	4	5
Total	100	100	100	100	100	100	100	100	100	100	100	100
(n)	(74)	(323)	(10)	(121)	(241)	(14)	(106)	(17)	(41)	(3)	(194)	(1144)

Questionnaire 3, question 1: Please state your major activities since Jan. 1st 1992.

About three-quarters of employed graduates reported no limitation with respect to the duration of the work contract, 24 per cent stated fixed term contracts, 1 per cent weekly or monthly renewable contracts, and 2 per cent other conditions of time-limitation. Fixed term contracts were most common in connection with part-time employment (57 per cent). The average duration of these contracts was 22 months. As Figure 4.1 indicates, permanent work contracts were most often reported by graduates from business studies (87 per cent) and engineering (80 per cent). On the other hand, less than half of the graduates from communication sciences, geography/geology, agriculture, education/teacher training, medical fields and humanities stated permanent employment contracts five years after the ERASMUS-supported study period abroad. Because of the small numbers in most of these fields of study random effects could not be excluded.

Table 4.4

Status of Graduates at the Time of the Third Survey, by Field of Study During the ERASMUS-Supported Period of Study Abroad 1988/89 (per cent of graduates responding five years after the ERASMUS study period)

	Field of study*																Total
	Agr	Arc	Art	Bus	Edu	Eng	Geo	Hum	Lan	Law	Mat	Med	Nat	Soc	Com	Other	
Full-time employed	62	70	60	87	75	83	45	62	72	80	79	86	55	73	50	71	78
Education/training (without employment)	8	6	10	2	8	3	27	8	5	4	6	0	21	5	17	4	5
Education/training and full-time employment	0	0	0	0	0	1	0	0	1	2	0	0	4	0	0	2	1
Education/training and part-time employment	0	0	0	0	0	0	0	3	1	2	3	0	6	3	0	4	1
Part-time employment (without education/training)	8	12	20	3	17	4	27	3	11	4	9	0	9	0	33	6	6
Unemployed	8	3	0	3	0	2	0	8	7	2	0	0	2	11	0	12	4
Other	15	9	10	5	0	7	0	18	2	7	3	14	4	8	0	0	5
Total	100	100	100	100	100	100	100	100	100	100	100	100	100	100	100	100	100
(n)	(13)	(33)	(10)	(396)	(12)	(123)	(11)	(39)	(184)	(131)	(33)	(14)	(53)	(37)	(6)	(49)	(1144)

Questionnaire 3, question 1: Please state your major activities since Jan. 1st 1992.

* Explanation see Table 3.8.

Of those employed at the time of third survey, actually 81 per cent were active in the country they studied in prior to the ERASMUS-supported period (i.e. in most cases their home country), 9 per cent were employed in the host country of the ERASMUS study period, 10 per cent were employed in a third country.

Figure 4.1
Duration of Employment Contract Held at the Time of the Third Survey, by Field of Study* During the ERASMUS-Supported Study Period Abroad 1988/89 (per cent of employed graduates responding five years after the ERASMUS study period)

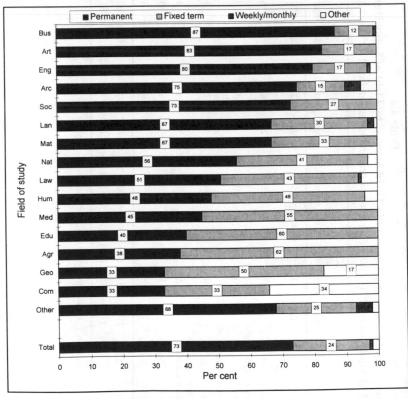

Questionnaire 3, question 3.3: Please state the duration of your current employment.

* Explanation see Table 3.8

Figure 4.2
Country of Employment Held at the Time of the Third Survey –
Where Different from Home Country, by Host Country (per cent of
employed graduates responding five years after the ERASMUS-supported
study period)

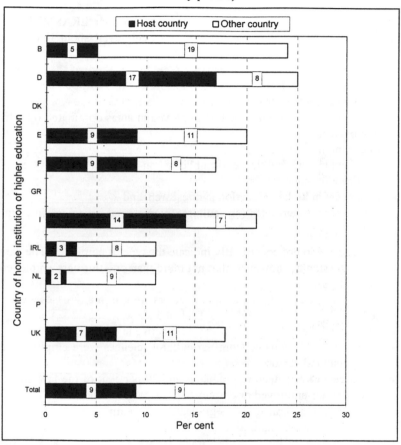

Questionnaire 3, question 1: Please state your major activities since Jan. 1st 1992.

As Figure 4.2 shows, Germany is the country absorbing the largest proportions of former ERASMUS students. These figures are similar to those
almost three years after the ERASMUS-supported period abroad. International mobility of former ERASMUS students in terms of working in a
foreign country largely depends on the duration of the period abroad. The
respective proportions ranged from 12 per cent among graduates who

spent at most three months in the host country to about 33 per cent whose stay abroad was longer than one year.

4.3 Employment Status and Sector of Employment

When asked to state the sector of employment, former ERASMUS students were provided 11 categories. Of those employed about five years after the ERASMUS-supported period,

- 24 per cent were active in industry,
- 17 per cent in commerce,
- 13 per cent in other private services,
- 9 per cent were self-employed or employed in areas dominated by self-employed professionals,
- 7 per cent in government,
- 5 per cent in other public, semi-public or non-profit-making services,
- 7 per cent in schools,
- 13 per cent in higher education and research, and
- 5 per cent in other areas (agriculture, international organizations, others).

The categories do not consistently indicate the type of employer. The data allow us to estimate, however, that not more than one-third are employed in the public sector.

As one might expect, employment sectors were in many cases clearly linked to certain fields of study. As Table 4.5 shows,

- 59 per cent of employed engineers were active in industry,
- 46 per cent of graduates from agricultural sciences were employed in the agricultural sector,
- 42 per cent of architecture graduates and 29 per cent of the law graduates were self-employed or employed in respective offices,
- 43 per cent of natural sciences graduates were employed in higher education and research institutions,
- 32 per cent of business studies graduates went to industry and 31 per cent to commerce.

Not all the findings might have been expected, though. More than half of the few education graduates employed at that stage were active at higher education and research institutions. Social science graduates were most widely spread over various sectors of the employment system. More graduates from foreign languages were employed in industry, commerce and other private services than in the education and research sector.

Table 4.5
Sector of Employment Held at the Time of the Third Survey, by Field of Study During the ERASMUS-Supported Study Period Abroad 1988/89 (per cent of employed graduates responding five years after the ERASMUS study period)

	Field of study*																Total
	Agr	Arc	Art	Bus	Edu	Eng	Geo	Hum	Lan	Law	Mat	Med	Nat	Soc	Com	Other	
Agriculture	46	0	0	0	0	0	0	0	1	0	0	0	0	0	0	2	1
Industry	0	3	0	32	0	59	11	6	14	6	33	8	31	9	0	8	24
Commerce/finance/insurance	0	3	10	31	0	2	0	12	16	8	18	0	2	18	0	14	17
Higher education or research institution	23	9	20	4	62	16	33	12	14	11	33	23	43	21	0	18	13
Primary, secondary or other school	8	3	10	2	31	2	33	21	24	1	3	0	2	15	33	6	7
National or regional government	8	21	10	3	0	2	0	15	5	26	0	23	4	12	17	6	7
Semi-public organization	0	3	0	3	0	4	0	0	1	1	0	23	4	6	0	4	3
Private non-profit org.	0	6	0	2	0	0	0	6	2	5	0	0	2	3	0	2	2
International, intergovernmental organization	0	0	0	2	0	2	0	0	4	3	0	0	0	3	0	0	2
Private services	8	9	40	18	0	8	0	6	13	7	9	0	8	9	17	22	13
Professional occupation (e.g. lawyer, medical doctor etc.)	0	42	10	3	8	4	11	6	5	29	3	23	4	6	33	10	9
Other	8	0	0	1	0	2	11	18	1	3	0	0	0	0	0	6	2
Total	100	100	100	100	100	100	100	100	100	100	100	100	100	100	100	100	100
(n)	(13)	(33)	(10)	(386)	(13)	(119)	(9)	(34)	(180)	(126)	(33)	(13)	(49)	(34)	(6)	(49)	(1107)

Questionnaire 3, question 4.1: In which sector are you currently employed?
* Explanation see Table 3.8.

Table 4.6
Sector of Employment Held at the Time of the Third Survey, by Country of Home Institution of Higher Education (per cent of employed graduates responding five years after the ERASMUS-supported study period)

	Country of home institution											Total
	B	D	DK	E	F	GR	I	IRL	NL	P	UK	
Agriculture	0	0	0	0	2	0	0	0	5	0	2	1
Industry	16	33	25	14	28	0	13	28	0	0	25	24
Commerce/finance/insurance	13	15	25	21	19	14	8	17	8	0	22	17
Higher education or research institution	27	14	25	13	6	29	21	11	20	67	8	13
Primary, secondary or other school	1	3	0	24	10	14	5	11	5	33	6	7
National or regional government	8	9	0	10	3	0	5	11	18	0	8	7
Semi-public organization	0	2	13	2	3	0	4	0	3	0	4	3
Private non-profit organization	4	1	0	1	3	0	2	0	10	0	2	2
International, intergovernmental organization	3	1	0	4	3	0	2	0	0	0	1	2
Private services	7	15	13	5	16	0	20	6	20	0	10	13
Professional occupation (e.g. lawyer, medical doctor etc.)	19	4	0	3	7	43	19	17	13	0	11	9
Other	3	2	0	5	1	0	2	0	0	0	2	2
Total	100	100	100	100	100	100	100	100	100	100	100	100
(n)	(75)	(319)	(8)	(109)	(232)	(14)	(101)	(18)	(40)	(3)	(188)	(1107)

Questionnaire 3, question 4.1: In which sector are you currently employed?

As Table 4.6 shows, a relatively large proportion of Dutch former ERASMUS students took over jobs in national, regional or local government. The largest proportion of those employed in educational and research institutions was among Portuguese, Greek, Italian, Spanish and Belgian respondents. Of the remaining countries, more than half of the former ERASMUS students were employed in industry, commerce and private services. These findings can be explained in part, but obviously not completely by the composition of ERASMUS students of the various countries according to field of study.

Twenty-six per cent of those graduates who were employed in private enterprises estimated the number of employees in the enterprise as at most 50. A further 29 per cent were employed in enterprises with 51 to 500 employees, 10 per cent estimated the number of employees between 501 and 1,000, 18 per cent between 1,000 and 10,000, and finally 17 per cent estimated the number of employees at more than 10,000. Employment in small enterprises (i.e. up to 50 employees) were most common among graduates from Greece, the Netherlands, Italy and Spain (see Table 4.7). On the other hand, more than half of graduates from Ireland, Germany and Denmark who worked in enterprises reported more than 500 employees.

Table 4.7
Number of Employees in the Enterprise Employing the Respondent, by Country of Home Institution of Higher Education (mean of responses by employed graduates responding five years after the ERASMUS-supported study period)

	Country of home institution										Total
	B	D	DK	E	F	GR	I	IRL	NL	UK	
Up to 50	26	19	14	37	27	75	43	10	46	24	26
51 – 100	14	6	0	15	4	0	6	0	12	6	7
101 – 200	7	6	0	15	14	0	12	20	8	14	11
201 – 500	14	11	29	7	10	0	8	10	15	13	11
501 – 1000	12	11	14	12	8	0	6	0	0	13	10
1,001 – 10,000	26	22	0	14	18	0	12	20	19	17	18
10,001 and more	2	25	43	0	19	25	14	40	0	13	17
Total	100	100	100	100	100	100	100	100	100	100	100
(n)	(43)	(205)	(7)	(59)	(153)	(4)	(51)	(10)	(26)	(134)	(692)

Questionnaire 3, question 4.11: If you are employed in an enterprise please estimate the number of employees.

Chapter 5

The European and International Dimension of Transition to Work

5.1 Criteria of Graduates when Seeking Employment

Former ERASMUS students were asked to state the importance (on a scale from 1 = "very important" to 5 = "not at all important") of several criteria when seeking employment. Most of the 10 items stated in the questionnaire were taken from a survey of German graduates which was conducted by the Kassel Centre in the 1980s. Some items were added to evaluate the possible international orientation of former ERASMUS students. Eventually, five categories of job-related orientations were represented by the various items:

(1) contents of work (possibility of personal development, opportunity to realize own ideas, accomplishing sensible/useful professional tasks);

(2) status and career (high employment security, well recognized professional status, high income);

(3) professional competence (applying knowledge and skills acquired while studying);

(4) international dimensions of work assignment (applying foreign language skills, working in a foreign country);

(5) non-professional activities (enough spare time for other than professional activities).

The single items of two categories stood out clearly in their importance for graduates while seeking employment. On the one hand criteria concerned with the inclination to shape the content of one's own work and on the other hand the possibility of applying one's professional competence:

- 83 per cent of graduates stated the possibility of personal development as an important criterion,
- 76 per cent mentioned the application of knowledge and skills acquired while studying,

- 69 per cent mentioned the opportunity to realize their own ideas, and
- 67 per cent wanted to accomplish sensible/useful professional activities.

Figure 5.1
Importance of Criteria for Former ERASMUS Students when Seeking Employment (per cent* of employed graduates responding five years after the ERASMUS-supported study period)

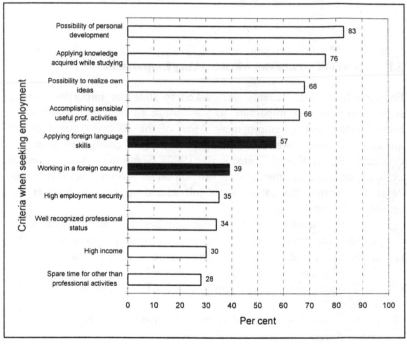

Questionnaire 3, question 4.2: What criteria were important for you when seeking employment?

* Categories 1 and 2 on a scale from 1 = "very important" to 5 = "not at all important"

Criteria related to the international dimension of work did not play the most important role for former ERASMUS students when seeking employment, as Figure 5.1 shows. However, a majority of respondents stated the application of foreign language skills as an important criterion (57 per cent). Notably high as well was the proportion (39 per cent) of graduates who mentioned working in a foreign country as an important criterion when seeking employment.

Criteria related to the international dimension of work played a more important role for former ERASMUS students than status and career motives as well as a more important role than issues of job security and spare time for non-professional activities. Only about one-third of former ERASMUS students mentioned high employment security, well recognized professional status or high income as important criteria when seeking employment. A balance between professional and non-professional activities was desired by 29 per cent of the graduates who stated enough spare time for other than professional activities as an important criterion.

Table 5.1

Importance of Criteria when Seeking Employment, by Duration of the ERASMUS-Supported Study Period Abroad 1988/89 (per cent* of employed graduates responding five years after the ERASMUS study period)

	Duration of study period abroad in months				Total
	3 or less	4 – 6	7 – 12	13 and more	
Applying knowledge and skills acquired while studying	76	74	78	70	76
High income	24	27	35	46	30
Accomplishing sensible/useful professional activities	71	64	66	65	66
Enough spare time for other than professional activities	32	25	30	28	28
Possibility of personal development	83	83	82	84	83
Possibility to realize own ideas	73	67	67	69	68
Well recognized professional status	33	33	35	44	34
High employment security	40	34	35	26	35
Applying foreign language skills	40	59	64	63	57
Working in a foreign country	27	36	44	59	39

Questionnaire 3, question 4.2: What criteria were important to you when seeking employment?

* Categories 1 and 2 on a scale from 1 = "very important" to 5 = "not at all important"

As one might expect, the importance of an international dimension of employment is influenced by the duration of the study period abroad: the longer the study period abroad lasted, the more former ERASMUS students mentioned the application of foreign language skills or working in a foreign country as important criteria when seeking employment (see Table 5.1). Application of foreign language skills was mentioned as an important criterion by 40 per cent of graduates who went abroad for three months, by 59 per cent of those who spent four to six months in the host country, and by 64 per cent of those who stayed more than half a year abroad. This finding reflects the foreign language competence of former ERASMUS students which is strongly related to the duration of the period abroad. About two-thirds of the respondents who rated their own language competence after the ERASMUS-supported period abroad 1988/89 as high or very high viewed the application of this competence as important when seeking employment. The respective proportion was less than one-third among those former ERASMUS students who stated average or lesser foreign language abilities.

The longer the ERASMUS-supported period abroad lasted, the more the students intended to find employment in a foreign country. Among the respondents who spent more than a year in the ERASMUS host country, 59 per cent mentioned this issue as an important criterion while seeking employment. On the other hand, the respective proportion was only 27 per cent among those who went abroad for at most three months. Former ERASMUS students who went to the smaller European countries with not widely used languages stated international criteria less often than former students who stayed for a period abroad in the larger European countries. As Table 5.2 shows, the proportion of students who stated applying of foreign language skills or working in a foreign country as important criteria while seeking employment was clearly above average in the case of former students who had spent their study period in Portugal, Denmark, Greece, the Netherlands and Belgium. Highest importance of international criteria was stated by former ERASMUS students who spent their study period abroad in Spain or the United Kingdom.

As one might expect, the application of foreign language skills is most often seen by former students of foreign languages as an important criterion in seeking employment (80 per cent). The respective proportion was also above average as well on the part of graduates from business studies (62 per cent) and engineering (58 per cent). At least in the case of business studies the high importance of this criterion could be explained by the above-average duration of the period abroad and the correspondingly high language competence after the period abroad. Former students of business studies also most often intended to find employment in a foreign country (47 per cent). Among former ERASMUS students in architecture, art and design as well as in medical fields the international criteria of employment played only a minor role (see Table 5.3). The proportion of respondents stating the application of foreign language skills as an important criterion while seeking a job was less than 10 per cent in medical fields as well as in art and design. Only 8 per cent of graduates from medical fields stated work in a foreign country as an important criterion for their search.

Table 5.2

Importance of Criteria when Seeking Employment, by Host Country
(per cent* of employed graduates responding five years after the
ERASMUS-supported study period)

	Host country											Total
	B	D	DK	E	F	GR	I	IRL	NL	P	UK	
Applying knowledge and skills acquired while studying	67	79	67	79	78	58	75	65	74	75	75	76
High income	0	31	17	24	32	32	37	33	30	27	31	30
Accomplishing sensible/useful professional activities	92	75	67	71	69	79	63	66	62	55	60	67
Enough spare time for other than professional activities	25	34	67	30	31	28	39	17	25	27	23	28
Possibility of personal development	88	82	83	82	84	84	90	83	85	82	81	83
Possibility to realize own ideas	67	62	67	68	69	63	73	64	85	82	68	69
Well recognized professional status	33	41	17	32	34	0	41	28	29	36	35	34
High employment security	42	33	50	35	41	21	34	28	37	36	32	35
Applying foreign language skills	38	59	17	70	61	37	47	54	33	9	60	57
Working in a foreign country	17	41	0	46	38	21	34	40	26	27	43	39

Questionnaire 3, question 4.2: What criteria were important to you when seeking employment?

* Categories 1 and 2 on a scale from 1 = "very important" to 5 = "not at all important"

Table 5.3

Importance of Criteria When Seeking Employment, by Field of Study During the ERASMUS-Supported Study Period Abroad 1988/89 (per cent* of employed graduates responding five years after the ERASMUS study period)

	Field of study** during study period abroad																Total
	Agr	Arc	Art	Bus	Edu	Eng	Geo	Hum	Lan	Law	Mat	Med	Nat	Soc	Com	Other	
Applying knowledge and skills acquired while studying	85	79	89	73	75	77	67	91	75	83	61	85	76	75	100	67	76
High income	8	10	20	41	18	34	22	16	24	26	21	38	27	24	33	20	30
Accomplishing sensible/useful professional activities	85	88	75	61	83	61	89	77	62	75	63	92	63	83	100	65	67
Enough spare time for other than professional activities	8	31	70	25	73	24	33	25	37	27	24	8	36	29	50	23	28
Possibility of personal development	77	88	90	85	83	81	78	82	76	86	88	85	77	86	100	82	83
Possibility to realize own ideas	54	81	80	69	91	68	44	84	61	66	76	69	66	74	100	72	69
Well recognized professional status	31	34	33	38	45	31	0	17	30	33	30	38	40	32	83	43	34
High employment security	38	19	20	35	27	39	22	42	43	27	33	38	39	15	50	40	35
Applying foreign language skills	31	19	0	62	50	58	33	24	80	54	27	8	56	46	33	57	57
Working in a foreign country	15	27	20	47	18	38	11	13	39	40	23	8	34	44	17	36	39

Questionnaire 3, question 4.2: What criteria were important to you when seeking employment?

* Categories 1 and 2 on a scale from 1 = "very important" to 5 = "not at all important"

** Explanation see Table 3.8.

The findings of this survey suggest that the application of foreign language skills is a more important motivation among women than among men. As Table 5.4 shows, 65 per cent of women stated this criteria as important while seeking employment as compared to 49 per cent of the men. By controlling a possible impact of the composition of male and female students according to field of study, we note that, with the exception of social sciences, female respondents in each field of study stated the importance of applying foreign language skills more often than male respondents. On the other hand, no differences between male and female respondents could be observed regarding the stated importance of working in a foreign country as a criterion while seeking employment.

Table 5.4

Importance of Criteria when Seeking Employment, by Gender (per cent* of employed graduates responding five years after the ERASMUS-supported study period)

	Gender		Total
	Female	Male	
Applying knowledge and skills acquired while studying	79	72	76
High income	24	37	30
Accomplishing sensible/useful professional activities	69	64	66
Enough spare time for other than professional activities	34	23	28
Possibility of personal development	82	84	83
Possibility to realize own ideas	67	70	69
Well recognized professional status	35	34	34
High employment security	40	30	35
Applying foreign language skills	65	49	57
Working in a foreign country	38	39	39

Questionnaire 3, question 4.2: What criteria were important to you when seeking employment?

* Categories 1 and 2 on a scale from 1 = "very important" to 5 = "not at all important"

5.2 Criteria of Employers When Hiring Former ERASMUS Students

It would also be interesting in the context to know the weight employers put on European and international aspects in recruiting students. As only former students were surveyed and not employers, the former ERASMUS students who had graduated and subsequently were employed all the time or for at least some period were asked to state the importance (on a scale from 1 = "very important" to 5 = "not important at all") of various aspects possibly relevant for their current employers' decision to hire them. In using this method we have to take into account that it will provide only information on the perceived importance of aspects on the part of the students. It could be assumed that the candidates usually were not informed well by their employers about the reasons why they were hired. The perceived importance of the various aspects depends to a large extent on the attention the employers had paid to it in the course of the job interviews. Although we might expect that the perceptions stated by graduates will grasp reality to some extent, we cannot exclude the possibility that an employers' survey would have shown different results.

In response to the list of 13 items provided in the questionnaire, former ERASMUS students perceived the following criteria (in order of frequency) as important or very important to employers when hiring them:
- personality and social behaviour (82 per cent),
- foreign language competence (64 per cent),
- specialization within field of study (60 per cent),
- the study period abroad (53 per cent),
- examination results, i.e. grades (49 per cent),
- vocational training (49 per cent),
- non-prolongation of the study programme (28 per cent),
- reputation of the home institution of higher education (27 per cent),
- reputation of teaching staff, notably professors (17 per cent),
- reputation of the ERASMUS host institution of higher education (15 per cent),
- gender (13 per cent),
- world view/philosophical, religious or political ideas (13 per cent), and
- social background/family background (12 per cent).

An analysis of the intercorrelations or of the factor structures shows that most of the items are independent, i.e. not correlated with other aspects. Only two dimensions emerged with two or more correlated items:

(1) international competences, i.e. foreign language competence and study period abroad;
(2) reputation of institutions of higher education and teaching staff.

Table 5.5

Importance of Aspects in Employers' Decision to Hire the Respondents, by Country of Home Institution of Higher Education
(per cent* of employed graduates responding five years after the ERASMUS-supported study period)

	\multicolumn{11}{c}{Country of home institution}	Total
	B	D	DK	E	F	GR	I	IRL	NL	P	UK	
Specialization within field of study	61	61	50	75	59	89	63	76	69	100	43	60
Vocational training	57	44	75	70	33	38	61	50	63	100	47	49
Foreign language competence	72	59	88	74	75	70	62	36	53	0	53	64
Non-prolongation of the study programme	25	42	0	19	18	50	29	0	24	0	10	28
Personality and social behaviour	89	84	88	73	86	56	69	65	85	67	83	81
Gender	12	12	20	21	19	17	13	7	0	0	9	13
Social background/ family background	14	9	0	13	26	11	7	13	9	0	8	12
Reputation of the home institution	42	16	13	53	35	38	31	40	13	0	17	27
Study period abroad	56	61	88	63	61	60	42	25	50	0	33	53
Reputation of the ERASMUS host institution	29	7	29	37	17	22	14	13	6	0	10	15
Examination results (grades)	70	52	38	47	20	44	53	82	49	67	59	49
Reputation of teaching staff/ professor	23	12	0	29	14	70	35	43	9	33	8	17
World view/philo-sophical, religious or political ideas	25	9	14	18	12	14	23	17	8	0	12	13

Questionnaire 3, question 4.6: All things considered, how do you rate the importance of the following aspects regarding your current (or last) employer's decision to hire you?

* Categories 1 and 2 on a scale from 1 = "very important" to 5 = "not at all important"

Altogether, former ERASMUS students were obviously convinced that their international competences were key criteria in the view of the employers hiring them. Foreign languages was stated as the second and study experience abroad as the fourth most important among 13 criteria mentioned. Irrespective of what the criteria for most graduates might be, the majority of former ERASMUS students got the impression that they were sought for because of their specific international competences and experiences.

As Table 5.5 shows, foreign language competence and studying abroad for some period were mentioned most often as an important criterion for employers by former ERASMUS students from Denmark, Spain and France. On the other hand, the respective proportions were surprisingly low among former students from Ireland and the United Kingdom. Only 25 per cent of the Irish and 33 per cent of the British respondents stated that in their view the ERASMUS-supported period abroad was an important criterion for their employers in hiring them. Although the foreign language proficiency was assessed by somewhat more Irish and British respondents as important for the employers (36 per cent and 53 per cent), the respective proportions in most other countries were clearly higher.

Former ERASMUS students who spent their period abroad in the smaller European countries, i.e. Belgium, Denmark, Greece and Portugal, were less convinced that their foreign language proficiency or studying for some period abroad were important criteria for their employers in hiring them (see Table 5.6). The highest proportion of former students who stated the importance of foreign language competence for the employers was surprisingly not among those who spent their period abroad in a country with English as the native language but among the respondents who stayed in Germany (72 per cent). This might reflect the fact that the highest proportion of former host students were eventually employed in Germany.

As one might expect, foreign language competences are considered most important by students in foreign languages (84 per cent). Few former students in medical fields (10 per cent), art and design (14 per cent) and architecture (25 per cent) stated that they perceived their foreign language proficiency as an important criterion for their employers in hiring them (see Table 5.7). None of the former students in agriculture and geography/geology stated that the period abroad was an important criterion for the employer.

Table 5.6

Importance of Aspects in Employers' Decision to Hire the Respondents, by Host Country (per cent* of employed graduates responding five years after the ERASMUS-supported study period)

	B	D	DK	E	F	GR	I	IRL	NL	P	UK	Total
						Host country						Total
Specialization within field of study	63	56	33	56	55	56	63	56	65	78	65	60
Vocational training	35	51	75	46	48	27	60	40	55	38	50	49
Foreign language competence	39	72	0	67	61	33	63	63	52	33	68	64
Non-prolongation of the study programme	33	11	0	34	28	0	16	23	26	0	36	28
Personality and social behaviour	78	80	80	82	83	76	85	69	86	70	81	81
Gender	0	13	0	14	11	20	17	11	14	0	15	13
Social background/ family background	0	12	0	16	8	6	10	4	17	13	17	12
Reputation of the home institution	20	32	25	23	26	12	31	21	33	30	26	27
Study period abroad	36	52	33	60	52	41	48	59	44	10	57	53
Reputation of the ERASMUS host institution	11	18	0	16	18	6	20	18	20	0	10	15
Examination results (grades)	57	42	75	54	54	39	57	44	46	56	45	49
Reputation of teaching staff/professor	23	17	25	20	16	20	16	14	22	38	15	17
World view/philosophical, religious or political ideas	22	16	0	12	13	13	5	16	24	14	13	13

Questionnaire 3, question 4.6: All things considered, how do you rate the importance of the following aspects regarding your current (or last) employer's decision to hire you?

* Categories 1 and 2 on a scale from 1 = "very important" to 5 = "not at all important"

The duration of the ERASMUS-supported study period abroad is clearly correlated with the perceived importance of international competences. Whereas only about half of former ERASMUS students who went abroad for three months (or in some cases less) stated foreign language profi-

Table 5.7
Importance of Aspects in Employers' Decision to Hire the Respondents, by Field of Study During the ERASMUS-Supported Study Period Abroad 1988/89 (per cent* of employed graduates responding five years after the ERASMUS study period)

	Field of study**																Total
	Agr	Arc	Art	Bus	Edu	Eng	Geo	Hum	Lan	Law	Mat	Med	Nat	Soc	Com	Oth	
Specialization within field of study	85	65	78	58	73	56	71	63	53	67	63	83	61	66	83	52	60
Vocational training	42	60	40	49	78	39	43	53	47	45	79	73	38	57	80	46	49
Foreign language competence	46	25	17	67	55	59	22	52	84	63	41	10	54	63	60	59	64
Non-prolongation of the study programme	11	13	20	36	17	29	25	22	16	24	18	67	34	24	40	11	28
Personality and social behaviour	58	64	75	88	71	83	56	80	76	79	70	92	76	84	80	84	81
Gender	0	14	17	12	17	12	29	29	17	7	0	27	9	15	40	15	13
Social or family background	17	4	20	12	0	9	13	13	17	11	9	18	12	14	40	11	12
Reputation of the home institution	20	40	33	25	0	30	14	35	20	34	26	33	27	20	80	25	27
Study period abroad	50	25	0	59	40	56	22	42	56	57	50	45	48	48	20	36	53
Reputation of the ERASMUS host institution	0	12	14	11	17	14	0	25	18	24	17	20	9	24	50	11	15
Examination results (grades)	38	47	38	45	42	46	43	54	50	64	52	62	57	45	40	41	49
Reputation of teaching staff/ professor	0	37	33	9	50	15	13	27	17	26	30	55	38	7	33	8	17
World view/philosophical, religious or political ideas	0	29	33	10	29	11	33	15	14	19	0	42	6	11	50	18	13

Questionnaire 3, question 4.6: All things considered, how do you rate the importance of the following aspects regarding your current (or last) employer's decision to hire you?

*   Categories 1 and 2 on a scale from 1 = "very important" to 5 = "not at all important"

** Explanation see Table 3.8.

ciency as important for their employers, the respective proportion was about two-thirds, if the respondents had studied abroad for 4 to 12 months, and three-quarters, if study abroad lasted more than one year. The importance of a study period abroad for being hired varied similarly: one-third among those who spent three months abroad considered it important, slightly more than one half of those who went abroad for 4 to 12 months, and about two-thirds of those staying abroad for more than one year.

The international dimension was indirectly addressed in items referring to the role the reputation of the host institution of higher education might have played in the employers' decision to hire former students. According to the respondents, the reputation of the home institution, host institution and teaching staff did not play an outstanding role in this respect. On average, only about one in five reported aspects of reputation as important. The reputation of both the home and the host institutions of higher education seems to have played the most important role in Spain (53 per cent and 37 per cent respectively) and Belgium (41 per cent and 28 per cent). In addition, former Irish ERASMUS students (40 per cent) emphasized the role of the home institution and former Danish ERASMUS students (29 per cent) that of the host institution of higher education. Reputation of teaching staff was viewed most important in Greece (70 per cent) and Ireland (43 per cent). Only small differences could be observed by field of study regarding reputation of home institution and the ERASMUS host institution.

5.3 Applications and Job Offers in Foreign Countries

One of the most visible signs of an orientation to the international employment market is the attempt to find employment in a foreign country. As discussed elsewhere, 39 per cent of the former ERASMUS students stated working in a foreign country as an important criterion while seeking employment. About two-thirds of these graduates tried to realize their desire by applying for employment in countries different to their home country. Taking all respondents to the third questionnaire into account,

- 38 per cent of graduates applied for employment in a foreign country,
- 27 per cent received an offer of a job in a foreign country outside higher education,
- 7 per cent received an offer of a job at a higher education institution in a foreign country.

As one might expect, the proportion of former ERASMUS students who received an offer of a job in a foreign country was large among those who applied for a job inside or outside higher education (59 per cent). It is remarkable, though, that almost one-sixth of the respondents (15 per cent) received an offer of a job in a foreign country without any formal application.

As Table 5.8 shows, the proportion of graduates who applied for a job in a foreign country was largest among those from the small European countries. About three-quarters of the few Danish and two-thirds of the Irish respondents applied for a job in a foreign country. Above average proportions could be observed also among former ERASMUS students from Greece (43 per cent) and the Netherlands (41 per cent). Regarding the larger European countries, graduates from France (50 per cent) applied noticeably more often for employment in a foreign country than former students from Germany (33 per cent) or the United Kingdom (38 per cent).

Table 5.8

Proportion of Graduates Having Received Job Offers/Having Applied for a Job in a Foreign Country, by Country of Home Institution of Higher Education (per cent of employed graduates responding five years after the ERASMUS-supported study period)

	Country of home institution											Total
	B	D	DK	E	F	GR	I	IRL	NL	P	UK	
Application for employment abroad	27	34	75	28	51	43	41	61	41	0	37	39
Receipt of a job offer outside higher education from abroad	27	26	70	20	34	21	19	47	17	0	34	28
Receipt of a job offer in higher education from abroad	14	7	10	8	5	7	13	17	10	0	4	7
(n)	(74)	(314)	(10)	(120)	(232)	(14)	(105)	(18)	(40)	(3)	(191)	(1121)

Questionnaire 3, question 4.3: Did you apply for employment in a foreign country?

Questionnaire 3, question 4.4: Have you received an offer of a job (excluding a post in a higher education institution) in a foreign country?

Questionnaire 3, question 4.5: Have you received an offer to work in higher education in a foreign country?

Respondents from Denmark and Ireland who had applied most often in foreign countries received most frequently offers for jobs outside higher education (64 per cent and 50 per cent respectively). Irish respondents were more often offered a job at a higher education institution in a foreign country than former ERASMUS students from any other country.

The host country of the ERASMUS-supported study period seems to play an important role in the motivation of former students to apply in a foreign country. Former students who spent their period abroad in Denmark (none), Greece (26 per cent) and the Netherlands (31 per cent) stated less often that they applied for a job abroad. On the other hand former students who stayed in Germany (51 per cent), Belgium (48 per cent) and Spain (43 per cent) most often reported applications in foreign countries. There is no clear pattern in these findings. It seems that foreign language issues were of importance in that periods abroad in countries with lesser-known languages were less likely to lead to subsequent work abroad. Economic factors may also play a role as well as social ties established and lifestyles experienced during the period abroad.

Among the possible countries chosen by former ERASMUS students in their applications for employment, the ERASMUS host country was the most important one. Among those respondents who applied for a job in a foreign country,

• 44 per cent applied only in the host country,
• 8 per cent in the host country and in another EC country (or possibly more than one),
• 5 per cent in the host country and in a non-EC country, and
• 2 per cent in the host country, another EC country and a non-EC country.

Altogether, 59 per cent of the graduates who applied for employment abroad did so in their former host country. Obviously the experiences during the study period abroad had led for a remarkable proportion of students to a strong orientation and connection to the ERASMUS host country. This was especially the case among the former students enrolled for some period in Germany (76 per cent), France, Belgium (66 per cent each) and Spain (65 per cent).

Applications for employment only in EC countries different from the host country were mentioned by 18 per cent of the respective students. Only non-EC countries were chosen for their applications by 15 per cent of the respondents who applied for employment abroad. The most important non-EC country was the United States, where 8 per cent of the potential internationally mobile students applied.

The majority of respondents who received an offer of a job in a foreign country outside higher education did so from employers in their former host country (59 per cent). The respective proportion was highest among those who spent their period abroad in Germany (73 per cent), France (70 per cent) and Spain (66 per cent). Because the number of former ERASMUS host students who received an offer of a job in a foreign country was very small for most of the other EC countries, it is difficult to provide reliable figures on the role the host country, other EC countries or non-EC countries have played in this context.

Regarding fields of study, the highest proportion of graduates who applied for a job in a foreign country could be observed among those who studied in small fields not explicitly mentioned in the ERASMUS classification and therefore categorized as "other fields of study" (51 per cent). Other subject areas with relatively high proportions of applications are foreign language studies (43 per cent), business studies and social sciences (41 per cent each). On the other hand, the proportion of former ERASMUS students who applied for employment abroad was smallest among those in medical fields (20 per cent), architecture, and education and teacher training (21 per cent each). Receipt of an offer of a job outside higher education institutions were most often reported by former students in business studies (36 per cent), other fields of study (33 per cent), engineering and medical fields (29 per cent each).

Applying for employment in a foreign country is clearly correlated with the duration of the ERASMUS-supported study period abroad. Whereas only 28 per cent of former ERASMUS students who spent a period of three months (or in a few cases less) abroad stated application activities abroad, this proportion was 51 per cent among those who spent more than one year in their host country (see Table 5.9). The latter were also the most successful in receiving offers of a job abroad outside higher education (42 per cent). On the other hand, it should be noted that none of the former ERASMUS students who spent more than one year abroad received an offer of a job at a higher education institution in a foreign country (most of these students were enrolled in non-university higher education).

Male respondents did not apply more often than female respondents for employment abroad but received slightly more offers of a job outside higher education (30 per cent as compared to 25 per cent). This difference is attributable to the composition according to fields of study.

Table 5.9

Proportion of Graduates Having Received a Job Offer/Having Applied for a Job in a Foreign Country, by Duration of ERASMUS-Supported Study Period Abroad 1988/89 (per cent of employed graduates responding five years after the ERASMUS study period)

	Duration of study period abroad in months				Total
	3 or less	4 – 6	7 – 12	13 and more	
Application for employment abroad	28	38	43	52	39
Receipt of a job offer abroad outside higher education	20	28	30	43	28
Receipt of a job offer abroad in higher education	9	8	8	0	7
(n)	(246)	(378)	(408)	(83)	(1115)

Questionnaire 3, question 4.3: Did you apply for employment in a foreign country?

Questionnaire 3, question 4.4: Have you received an offer of a job (excluding a post in a higher education institution) in a foreign country?

Questionnaire 3, question 4.5: Have you received an offer to work in higher education in a foreign country?

Chapter 6

The European and International Dimemsion of Work Tasks and Related Competences

6.1 International Contacts

Asked about the international contacts of the organization, institution or company by which they were employed,

- 71 per cent of the respondents reported continuous contacts with other countries, and
- 49 per cent reported continuous contacts with their ERASMUS host country.

The highest proportion of former ERASMUS students mentioning continuous contacts of their organization with foreign countries could be observed in Belgium (86 per cent) and Germany (80 per cent) and the lowest in Italy (56 per cent) and Spain (58 per cent). Continuous contacts of the organization with the ERASMUS host country was least often mentioned by respondents who spent their period abroad in Denmark (none), Portugal, Ireland (20 per cent each), Greece (22 per cent) and Belgium (29 per cent). These are the countries which are smallest in size and economic power within the European Union.

Former students in business studies, engineering and natural sciences were most often employed in an organization with continuous contacts with other countries and with the ERASMUS host country (see Figure 6.1). About 80 per cent stated continuous contacts (1 or 2 on a scale from 1 = "continuously" to 5 = "not at all") of their organization with other countries. Relations to the ERASMUS host country were most often mentioned by graduates in business studies (63 per cent). Former students in art and design (40 per cent), architecture (44 per cent), agriculture, education/teacher training and communication sciences (50 per cent each) least often reported continuous contacts of their organizations with other countries.

Figure 6.1
Extent of Contacts of the Respondent's Organization, Institution or Company with Other Countries, by Field of Study During Period Abroad 1988/89 (per cent* of employed graduates responding five years after the ERASMUS-supported study period)

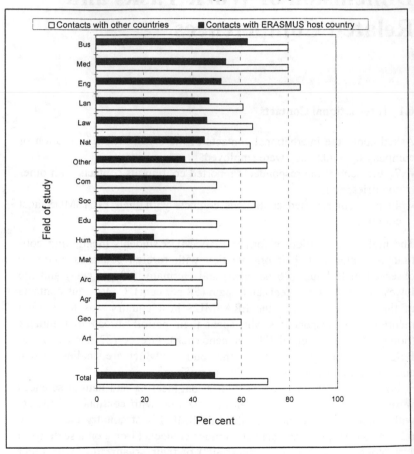

Questionnaire 3, question 4.7: To what extent does the organization, institution or company with which you are associated do business or have contact with other countries?

* Categories 1 and 2 on a scale from 1 = "continually" to 5 = "not at all"

Table 6.1

Extent of Contacts of Respondent's Organization, Institution or Company with Other Countries, by Sector of Employment (per cent of employed graduates responding five years after the ERASMUS-supported study period)

	Current employment sector*												Total
	Agr	Ind	Com	Hig	Pri	Nat	Sem	Non	Int	Ser	Pro	Oth	
Contacts with other countries													
1 = continually	22	83	71	62	14	25	41	57	100	61	38	47	60
2	22	7	7	19	9	12	17	22	0	10	17	18	11
3	22	6	9	13	29	20	7	4	0	11	20	0	12
4	33	3	6	2	28	21	21	9	0	8	13	24	9
5 = not at all	0	1	8	4	19	22	14	9	0	11	12	12	8
Total	100	100	100	100	100	100	100	100	100	100	100	100	100
Contacts with host country													
1 = continually	11	58	51	33	11	13	23	22	69	29	27	25	38
2	0	12	9	13	7	3	3	13	6	15	14	25	11
3	33	9	13	21	16	21	7	35	0	14	10	6	14
4	22	10	10	13	18	18	30	9	13	13	23	25	14
1 = not at all	33	11	17	21	49	45	37	22	13	29	26	19	23
Total	100	100	100	100	100	100	100	100	100	100	100	100	100
(n)	(9)	(262)	(183)	(135)	(76)	(76)	(30)	(23)	(16)	(140)	(92)	(16)	(1058)

Questionnaire 3, question 4.7: To what extent does the organisation, institution or company with which you are associated do business or have contact with other countries? Question 4.8: To what extent does the organization, institution or company with which you are associated do business or have contact with the host country of your ERASMUS study period abroad 1988/89?

* Explanation see Table 6.3

The longer the former ERASMUS students stayed abroad, the more often they reported continuous contacts of their organization with other countries and with the ERASMUS host country. As shown above, students who spent more time in the host country stated a high importance of the international dimension while seeking employment. Obviously, many found employment which suited them in this respect.

The frequency of international contacts varies according to the size of the organization in terms of the number of its employees. About 90 per cent of former ERASMUS students employed in organizations employing more than 1,000 persons stated continuous contacts of their enterprise with other countries. As Table 6.1 shows, international contacts of the organization also varied substantially by sector of employment. All respondents who were employed in international organizations stated continuous contacts of their organization with other countries. The respective proportion was 90 per cent among former ERASMUS students employed in industry, 81 per cent in higher education and 78 per cent each in commercial sectors and in private non-profit organizations. The respective quota was lowest in primary or secondary schools (23 per cent), national or regional governments (37 per cent) and in the agriculture sector (44 per cent).

6.2 Use of Competences Acquired Abroad

Obviously, both many former ERASMUS graduates seeking for jobs and most employers employing persons who had studied abroad expect a utilization on the job of the competences typically developed and reinforced by a study period in another country. This holds true, though one does neither expect study abroad to serve exclusively professional preparation nor the jobs to require exhaustive utilization of competences acquired abroad. However, as study abroad might have varied impacts on the students' competences, it is not possible to trace the professional utilization of the competences acquired abroad more or less comprehensively. As an approximation, former ERASMUS students were asked to state the extent to which in their job they use the host country language, knowledge about the host country and the knowledge in their field of study acquired abroad, and the frequency of travel abroad (on a scale from 1 = "continually" to 5 = "not at all"). Continual activities (scale points 1 or 2) were stated by

• 47 per cent in terms of listening and speaking in the host country language in work related activities,
• 47 per cent also in terms of writing and reading,

- 30 per cent as regards first hand professional knowledge about the host country,
- 30 per cent in terms of using first hand knowledge of the host culture and society,
- 17 per cent in terms of professional travel to the ERASMUS host country,
- 24 per cent in terms of professional travel to other foreign countries, and
- 37 per cent in terms of using knowledge in the field of study acquired abroad.

Figure 6.2
Use of Competences Acquired During the ERASMUS-Supported Period Abroad 1988/89 on the Job Five Years Later (per cent* of employed graduates responding five years after the ERASMUS study period)

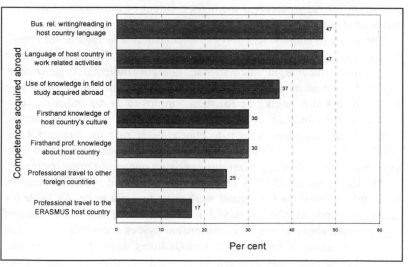

Questionnaire 3, question 4.9: To what extent do the responsibilities of your work involve the following?
* Categories 1 and 2 on a scale from 1 = "continually" to 5 = "not at all"

These findings suggest that many former ERASMUS students make continuous use of the competences they acquired during the study period abroad. There are also a considerable number of former ERASMUS students for whom this holds true only to a limited extent. For example, about one-fifth of the respondents stated that they did not use the host country language at all on the job. Also, more than one-quarter never made any professional use of knowledge about the host country. This suggests we should look more closely at the possible causes of a limited utilization of the competences acquired during the study period abroad.

As Table 6.2 indicates, former ERASMUS students who went to Belgium, Denmark, Greece and the Netherlands as well as the small numbers who went to Portugal made least frequent use of foreign language competence and professional knowledge about the host country, and were least frequently expected to undertake professional travel to the host country. Obviously, those who spent their study period in a small European country eventually have a lesser chance of making immediate use of the competences acquired abroad. Also respondents who had spent their ERASMUS-supported study period in Ireland and Italy reported a below-average use of their international competences. In contrast, former ERASMUS students who had spent their ERASMUS-supported study period in Germany perceived the highest extent of utilization of their international competences.

The sector of employment plays an important role as regards the opportunity of applying international competences. As one might aspect, former ERASMUS students in international, intergovernmental organizations reported most often a continuous use of those competences (see Table 6.3), but this also holds true for those employed in the industry, commerce, higher education or in primary or secondary schools. In contrast, international competences seem to play a lesser role for former ERASMUS students active in the agriculture sector, national or regional governments, semi-public organizations or private non-profit organizations.

The longer the ERASMUS-supported period abroad 1988/89 lasted, the more international the subsequent work tasks turn out to be. As Table 6.4 shows, respondents who had stayed in the host country for more than half a year stated above-average international activities across all items listed in the questionnaire. In respect to various items, highest use of international competences was reported by respondents who had spend more than one year of study abroad. As the duration of the period abroad is certainly associated with the level of competences acquired abroad, this finding also reinforces the view both that many former ERASMUS students tend to succeed in finding jobs and work tasks and that employers tend to succeed in selecting and allocating former ERASMUS students to a considerable extent in a way which provides the opportunities of making use of international competences acquired or reinforced during the study period abroad.

Regarding field of study, we note that graduates in foreign languages reported most often the use of foreign language proficiency (61 per cent) and the use of first hand information about the host country (45 per cent). Also graduates from business studies and education/teacher training reported above-average use of host country-related knowledge and competences. In contrast, respondents from agriculture, architecture, art and design, geography/geology and medical fields mentioned least frequent use of qualifications acquired abroad. No noteworthy variation in the use of international competences could be observed by home country or by gender of the respondents.

Former ERASMUS students were asked how strong they presently feel with respect to language and knowledge of the host country (on a scale from 1 = "very strong" to 5 = "very weak"). Thus some of the same items were used as those in questions referred to above on the work tasks.

Altogether, almost three-quarters each (73 per cent and 72 per cent respectively) of the respondents felt strongly (scale point 1 or 2) five years after graduation with regard to using the language of the ERASMUS host country both

- in work-related communication (i.e. telephone conversations, face-to-face discussions, etc.),
- in work-related writing and reading (business related memoranda, reports, etc.).

More than half of the respondents (57 per cent) felt strongly with regard to using first hand knowledge of the culture and society of the host country. The lowest proportion (46 per cent) felt strongly with regard to using first-hand professional knowledge about the host country.

This question was linked to that on work tasks in order to examine whether those assigned international work tasks consider themselves especially well qualified in those areas. In fact, work tasks and self-rating of competence are highly correlated. Correlation coefficients were about .7 regarding the use and proficiency of language competence and about .6 regarding the applying and availability of knowledge about the host country. As shown above, the more qualified former ERASMUS students were in host country-related activities, the more they made use of it in their work. One should bear in mind, though, that the competences rated cannot be attributed predominantly to the study period abroad. They might have been acquired prior to the study period abroad and thereafter.

Table 6.2
Extent of Host Country-Related Activities in Job Held at the Time of the Third Survey, by Host Country
(per cent of employed graduates responding five years after the ERASMUS-supported study period)

	Host country											Total
	B	D	DK	E	F	GR	I	IRL	NL	P	UK	
Using the language of the host country in work related activities												
Continually (1+2)	19	53	20	44	45	33	32	56	17	0	56	47
Partly (3)	19	19	0	13	18	6	11	11	20	0	14	15
Rarely (4+5)	62	28	80	44	37	61	56	33	63	100	29	38
Writing/reading business related in host country language												
Continually (1+2)	19	52	20	40	42	39	27	53	22	9	59	47
Partly (3)	24	14	0	10	20	6	10	22	11	0	16	16
Rarely (4+5)	57	34	80	50	38	56	63	25	67	91	24	38
Using firsthand professional knowledge about the host country												
Continually (1+2)	17	43	0	32	29	11	21	17	29	0	31	30
Partly (3)	8	23	25	19	20	17	21	14	22	9	25	21
Rarely (4+5)	75	34	75	49	51	72	57	69	49	91	44	49
Using firsthand knowledge of the host culture and society												
Continually (1+2)	0	39	20	42	31	6	26	19	25	0	30	30
Partly (3)	25	22	20	15	20	29	26	14	20	9	28	23
Rarely (4+5)	75	38	60	44	49	65	48	67	55	91	42	47

(Table 6. 2 to be cont.)

(Table 6.2)	Host country											Total
	B	D	DK	E	F	GR	I	IRL	NL	P	UK	
Professional travel to the ERASMUS host country												
Continually (1+2)	0	27	0	20	19	6	12	8	9	0	16	17
Partly (3)	8	19	20	11	14	6	10	0	11	0	12	12
Rarely (4+5)	92	54	80	70	66	89	78	92	80	100	72	71
Professional travel to foreign countries other than the host country												
Continually (1+2)	13	25	20	17	23	35	32	19	24	10	27	24
Partly (3)	25	17	0	14	16	18	24	8	15	20	16	16
Rarely (4+5)	63	58	80	69	61	47	44	72	61	70	57	59
Using knowledge in the field of study acquired abroad												
Continually (1+2)	38	43	40	43	31	28	35	28	42	33	39	37
Partly (3)	13	28	0	18	29	28	20	36	25	22	26	26
Rarely (4+5)	50	29	60	40	39	44	45	36	33	44	35	37

Questionnaire 3, question 4.9: To what extent do the responsibilities of your work involve the following?

Table 6.3

Extent of Host Country-Related Activities in Job Held at the Time of the Third Survey, by Sector of Employment
(per cent of employed graduates responding five years after the ERASMUS-supported study period)

	Current employment sector												Total
	Agr	Ind	Com	Hig	Pri	Nat	Sem	Non	Int	Ser	Pro	Other	
Using the language of the host country in work-related activities													
Continually (1+2)	11	59	48	45	56	19	34	38	65	45	35	38	47
Partly (3)	22	14	19	18	6	10	14	14	18	13	22	19	15
Rarely (4+5)	67	27	32	36	38	71	52	48	18	42	43	44	38
Writing/reading business related in host country language													
Continually (1+2)	11	55	48	51	54	24	34	29	76	42	39	44	47
Partly (3)	11	16	14	17	12	14	10	10	6	17	25	19	16
Rarely (4+5)	78	29	37	32	34	63	55	62	18	42	37	38	38
Using firsthand professional knowledge about the host country													
Continually (1+2)	11	30	31	33	52	15	17	22	35	28	24	13	30
Partly (3)	11	29	18	15	13	18	14	17	24	28	19	38	21
Rarely (4+5)	78	41	51	52	35	68	69	61	41	44	56	50	49
Using firsthand knowledge of the host culture and society													
Continually (1+2)	0	32	32	29	56	12	24	22	41	30	21	25	30
Partly (3)	0	27	19	24	14	19	17	30	18	27	22	31	23
Rarely (4+5)	100	41	50	47	29	68	59	48	41	43	56	44	47

(Table 6.3 to be cont.)

(Table 6.3)

	Current employment sector												Total
	Agr	Ind	Com	Hig	Pri	Nat	Sem	Non	Int	Ser	Pro	Other	
Professional travel to the ERASMUS host country													
Continually (1+2)	0	23	19	16	14	5	14	9	24	16	14	13	17
Partly (3)	0	16	12	16	10	4	0	17	6	13	14	6	13
Rarely (4+5)	100	61	69	68	75	90	86	74	71	72	72	81	71
Professional travel to foreign countries other than the host country													
Continually (1+2)	0	36	28	20	8	9	14	13	41	25	18	19	24
Partly (3)	11	16	11	27	8	11	7	22	35	21	12	13	16
Rarely (4+5)	89	48	60	53	83	80	79	65	24	54	70	69	60
Using knowledge in the field of study acquired abroad													
Continually (1+2)	25	39	32	49	54	27	31	35	69	32	34	13	37
Partly (3)	38	30	31	21	18	23	17	9	6	24	26	50	26
Rarely (4+5)	38	31	38	30	28	51	52	57	25	44	40	38	37

Questionnaire 3, question 4.9: To what extent do the responsibilities of your work involve the following?

Agr = Agriculture
Ind = Industry
Com = Commerce/finance/insurance
Hig = Higher education institution or research establishment
Pri = Primary, secondary of other school
Nat = National or regional government

Sem = Semi-public organization
Non = Private non-profit organization
Int = International, intergovernmental organization (excluding private companies)
Ser = Private services
Pro = Professional occupation (e.g. lawyer, medical doctor etc.)

Table 6.4
Extent of Host Country-Related Activities in Job Held at the Time of the Third Survey, by Duration of the ERASMUS-Supported Study Period Abroad 1988/89 (per cent of employed graduates responding five years after the ERASMUS study period)

	Duration of study period abroad in months				Total
	3 or less	4 – 6	7 – 12	13 and more	
Using the language of the host country in work-related activities					
Continually (1+2)	31	49	53	59	47
Partly (3)	17	15	14	19	15
Rarely (4+5)	52	37	33	22	38
Writing/reading business-related in host country language					
Continually (1+2)	36	46	52	55	47
Partly (3)	18	15	13	20	16
Rarely (4+5)	46	39	34	24	38
Using firsthand professional knowledge about the host country					
Continually (1+2)	21	28	33	48	30
Partly (3)	16	22	23	27	22
Rarely (4+5)	63	50	44	26	49
Using firsthand knowledge of the host culture and society					
Continually (1+2)	18	29	35	46	30
Partly (3)	22	21	26	21	23
Rarely (4+5)	60	50	40	33	47
Professional travel to the ERASMUS host country					
Continually (1+2)	9	16	19	36	17
Partly (3)	9	14	13	15	13
Rarely (4+5)	83	70	68	49	70
Professional travel to foreign countries other than the host country					
Continually (1+2)	16	27	25	35	24
Partly (3)	17	15	15	22	16
Rarely (4+5)	67	57	60	43	59
Using knowledge in the field of study acquired abroad					
Continually (1+2)	31	35	40	55	37
Partly (3)	26	26	25	24	26
Rarely (4+5)	43	39	35	20	37

Questionnaire 3, question 4.9: To what extent do the responsibilities of your work involve the following?

6.3 Self-Rating of Competences

Five years after the ERASMUS-supported study period in another European country, former students were asked to rated some of their competences reinforced by the study period abroad: their knowledge of the host country as well as their competences in the language of the ERASMUS host country. In comparing the self-rating of those competences five years later to that immediately after the study period abroad, one might establish the long-term impact of studying abroad in those respects.

First, respondents were asked to rate their knowledge about the host country with regard to 12 aspects, notably regarding politics, culture and society, the economic system and geography as well as the higher education system of the host country. As Table 6.5 shows, former ERASMUS students considered their knowledge highest on the host country geography (2.3 on average on a scale from 1 = "extensive knowledge" to 5 = "very limited knowledge"), its higher education system (2.3), its customs and traditions (2.3 as well) and its social structure (2.4). On average of the 12 items, the ratings were 2.6.

The self-ratings of the knowledge of the host country five years after were on average .4 lower than shortly after the study period abroad. Former ERASMUS students obviously perceived a loss of knowledge over time, yet they continued to have a higher level of knowledge than they had, according to their ratings, prior to the study period abroad. The highest loss of knowledge over the years after the study period abroad was reported regarding dominant political issues of the host country.

An above-average decrease of knowledge was stated by respondents who had spent their study period abroad in Denmark (.9), Belgium (.7), Greece, Spain and the Netherlands (.5 each). Again, we note that the long-term impact of the study period seems to be lower by those who went to smaller European countries, and again Ireland turned out to be an exception.

The longer the duration of the study period abroad, the higher the knowledge of the host country turned out to be five years after graduation. However, the decrease of knowledge over the five years did not vary with the duration of the period abroad. Thus, the differences noted shortly after the study period abroad remained more or less constant over time.

Table 6.5

Knowledge About the ERASMUS Host Country Shortly After and Five Years After the ERASMUS-Supported Study Period Abroad 1988/89, by Host Country (mean* of respondents five years after the ERASMUS study period)

		Host country											Total
		B	D	DK	E	F	GR	I	IRL	NL	P	UK	
Political system and institutions	Shortly after	2.3	2.2	3.1	2.1	2.3	2.4	2.4	2.4	2.4	2.6	2.1	2.2
	Five years after	2.9	2.7	4.1	2.6	2.7	2.9	2.8	2.8	3.2	3.5	2.6	2.7
Dominant political issues	Shortly after	2.5	2.1	3.3	2.1	2.3	2.2	2.5	2.3	2.7	3.2	2.1	2.2
	Five years after	3.3	2.8	4.4	2.9	2.9	3.2	2.8	2.7	3.4	3.8	2.9	2.9
Foreign policy in general	Shortly after	2.7	2.4	3.9	2.4	2.6	2.7	2.8	2.7	2.9	3.8	2.3	2.5
	Five years after	3.5	3.0	4.3	3.1	2.9	3.3	3.2	3.1	3.4	4.2	2.9	3.0
Policy towards your own country	Shortly after	2.5	2.4	3.6	2.3	2.4	3.0	2.9	3.0	2.8	3.4	2.2	2.4
	Five years after	3.2	2.7	4.1	3.0	2.7	3.1	3.1	3.3	3.2	3.9	2.7	2.8
System of higher education	Shortly after	1.7	1.8	1.9	1.9	1.9	2.5	2.0	2.1	2.0	2.5	1.9	1.9
	Five years after	2.5	2.2	3.0	2.4	2.2	2.9	2.5	2.4	2.7	2.8	2.2	2.3
Cultural life (art, music, theatre, etc.)	Shortly after	2.1	2.2	2.6	1.8	2.1	2.4	2.1	1.9	2.2	2.2	2.1	2.1
	Five years after	2.8	2.5	3.4	2.2	2.3	2.8	2.3	2.3	2.6	2.6	2.5	2.4
Dominant social issues	Shortly after	2.0	2.1	3.1	2.0	2.3	2.5	2.3	2.1	2.4	2.5	2.1	2.2
	Five years after	3.0	2.5	4.0	2.6	2.6	3.1	2.6	2.5	2.9	3.3	2.7	2.6
Economic system	Shortly after	2.4	2.5	3.4	2.2	2.6	2.6	2.8	2.6	2.7	3.1	2.2	2.4
	Five years after	3.1	2.6	4.3	2.7	2.7	3.3	3.0	2.7	2.9	3.2	2.6	2.7
The country's geography	Shortly after	1.6	1.9	2.4	1.7	2.0	2.0	1.6	1.7	1.8	1.8	1.9	1.9
	Five years after	1.9	2.3	2.9	2.0	2.2	2.4	2.1	1.8	2.4	1.9	2.2	2.2

(Table 6.5 to be continued)

(Table 6.5)

						Host country							. Total
		B	D	DK	E	F	GR	I	IRL	NL	P	UK	
Social structure (family, class system)	Shortly after	2.1	2.1	2.4	1.8	2.3	2.6	1.9	1.9	2.1	2.3	2.1	2.1
	Five years after	2.8	2.4	3.6	2.2	2.4	2.9	2.2	2.2	2.5	2.9	2.4	2.4
Customs, traditions, religion	Shortly after	1.9	1.9	2.6	1.7	2.1	2.3	1.8	1.8	2.1	2.4	2.0	2.0
	Five years after	2.5	2.3	3.3	2.0	2.2	2.8	2.3	2.0	2.5	2.8	2.4	2.3
Sports, leisure/ recreational activities	Shortly after	2.3	2.2	2.7	2.1	2.3	2.4	2.2	2.0	2.6	2.8	2.1	2.2
	Five years after	2.8	2.5	3.6	2.6	2.5	2.8	2.6	2.4	2.6	3.0	2.5	2.6

Questionnaire 1, question 6.2: To what extent did you have significant problems in any of the following areas during your study period abroad?

Questionnaire 3, question 5.2: How would you rate your level of knowledge with regard to the following aspects of the host country?

* On a scale from 1 = "extensive knowledge" to 5 = "very limited knowledge"

Asked to rate their proficiency in the (major) language of instruction during the ERASMUS-supported study period abroad eventually five years thereafter, former ERASMUS students considered their foreign language competence – notably in reading and listening, but also in speaking and writing – as good, if the host country language was English, French, Spanish or German. In contrast, knowledge in Dutch, Greek, Portuguese and Danish was rated as low.

As Table 6.5 indicates, the ratings of the knowledge of the host country varied more strongly according to the respective language five years after than shortly after the study period abroad (though Table 6.6 does not refer to languages, but rather to host countries, this is in most cases indicative for the language of instruction). According to the former ERASMUS students who were taught in French, English, German, Spanish or Italian, their proficiency in the host country language five years later was more or less as good as it had been shortly after the study period abroad. In contrast, those who were taught at least in part in Dutch, Greek, Portuguese or Danish perceived a considerable loss of their proficiency in those languages. This finding does not come as a surprise, because those who had spent their study period abroad in the respective countries, less often stated opportunities to make use of their language proficiency on the job.

The relation between continuous use of foreign language in work-related activities and level of foreign language proficiency is shown in Table 6.7. Graduates who reported continuous use of the ERASMUS host country language in work-related activities, such as telephone conversations or face-to-face discussions, rated their foreign language proficiency five years after the period abroad on average higher than shortly after this study period (1.5 as compared to 1.8). Former ERASMUS students, however, who made use rarely or not at all of their language proficiency in employment, already stated a lower level of proficiency of the host country language shortly after the ERASMUS-supported period abroad and reported a considerable decrease of proficiency thereafter.

Table 6.6

Language Competence Shortly After and Five Years After the ERASMUS-Supported Study Period Abroad 1988/89, by Host Country (mean* of respondents five years after the ERASMUS study period)

		Host country											Total
		B	D	DK	E	F	GR	I	IRL	NL	P	UK	
Reading	Shortly after	2.6	2.0	4.4	1.7	1.9	2.1	2.4	1.8	2.4	3.0	1.7	1.9
	Five years after	3.1	1.9	5.3	1.8	1.7	4.4	2.4	1.7	4.2	4.1	1.6	1.9
Listening	Shortly after	2.5	1.9	4.3	1.6	1.9	2.1	2.1	1.8	2.4	3.3	1.8	1.9
	Five years after	3.4	2.0	5.6	1.9	1.9	4.3	2.4	1.9	4.3	4.8	1.9	2.1
Speaking	Shortly after	2.8	2.2	4.3	1.9	2.2	2.5	2.5	2.1	2.8	3.4	2.1	2.2
	Five years after	3.8	2.5	5.6	2.3	2.3	4.3	2.7	2.1	4.8	4.9	2.2	2.5
Writing	Shortly after	3.0	2.5	4.4	2.3	2.6	2.6	3.0	2.3	3.0	3.7	2.2	2.5
	Five years after	4.5	2.8	5.6	2.7	2.7	4.4	3.4	2.6	5.1	5.1	2.3	2.8

Questionnaire 1, question 4.7: How do you rate your competency in the (major) language of instruction at the host university (reply only if different from the language of instruction at your home university)?

Questionnaire 3, question 5.1: How do you rate your competence in the language of the ERASMUS host country (reply only if different from the language of your home country)?

* On a scale from 1 = "very good" to 5 = "extremely limited"

Table 6.7

Language Competence Shortly After the Period Abroad and Five Years Later, by use of Foreign Language in Employment (mean* of respondents five years after the ERASMUS-supported study period)

		Using the language of the host country in work-related activities					Total
		Continu-ally	2	3	4	Not at all	
Reading	Shortly after	1.6	1.8	1.9	2.1	2.4	1.9
	Five years after	1.3	1.6	1.9	2.2	3.1	2.0
Listening	Shortly after	1.6	1.8	1.9	2.0	2.4	1.9
	Five years after	1.4	1.7	2.2	2.4	3.3	2.1
Speaking	Shortly after	1.9	2.1	2.2	2.3	2.7	2.2
	Five years after	1.6	2.1	2.6	2.7	3.8	2.5
Writing	Shortly after	2.1	2.4	2.4	2.7	3.0	2.5
	Five years after	1.8	2.6	2.9	3.1	4.1	2.8

Questionnaire 1, question 4.7: How do you rate your competency in the (major) language of instruction at the host university (reply only if different from the language of instruction at your home university)?

Questionnaire 3, question 5.1: How do you rate your competence in the language of the ERASMUS host country (reply only if different from the language of your home country)?

* On a scale from 1 = "very good" to 5 = "extremely limited"

6.4 Ways of Keeping up Contact and Language Proficiency

Studying for some period abroad was not a short, coincidental experience for most of the participating students. Asked explicitly about the extent to which they kept contacts with the host country, former ERASMUS students responded 2.7 on a scale from 1 = "to a great extent" to 5 = "not at all".

In fact 49 per cent stated that they kept contact to a considerable extent (scale points 1 or 2) five years after the ERASMUS-supported period abroad. Two years earlier, 59 per cent had reported that they kept contact to a considerable extent. This indicates, as one might have expected, a certain loss over time in keeping contact.

Table 6.8
Extent of Continuation of Contacts with the ERASMUS Host Country, by Host Country (per cent and mean of respondents five years after the ERASMUS-supported study period)

	B	D	DK	E	F	GR	I	IRL	NL	P	UK	Total
1 = to a great extent	16	38	0	35	25	11	34	17	11	17	19	25
2	12	19	14	28	29	22	29	11	23	17	22	24
3	20	24	0	16	22	17	19	28	21	17	24	22
4	32	10	43	18	17	11	10	19	18	17	21	18
3 = not at all	20	8	43	4	7	39	8	25	28	33	14	12
Total	100	100	100	100	100	100	100	100	100	100	100	100
(n)	(25)	(144)	(7)	(107)	(320)	(18)	(79)	(36)	(57)	(12)	(397)	(1202)
Mean	3.3	2.3	4.1	2.3	2.5	3.4	2.3	3.3	3.3	3.3	2.9	2.7

Questionnaire 3, question 6.1: To what extent do you continue to keep contact with the ERASMUS host country?

As regards the respective host countries, notably those former ERASMUS students who spent their study period in Spain and Italy (63 per cent each), but also those had been in Germany (58 per cent) and France (54 per cent) continued to keep contact. As Table 6.8 shows, the respective proportion was lower among persons who had spent their study period abroad in the United Kingdom (41 per cent). These data suggest that, in addition to professional contacts as well as the frequency of international foreign language utilization and knowledge provision in general, cultural and tourism aspects come into play as well.

Less contact with the former host countries was reported by respondents who had spent their study period abroad in small European countries. Least contact was preserved with Denmark; also only a minority kept considerable contact with Belgium, Ireland, Greece, the Netherlands and Portugal. The data suggest that actively keeping contact to the host country does hardly compensate for infrequency of professional links to the host country, but is by and large mutually reinforcing.

The extent of contact kept up to five years after the study period abroad is clearly linked to the duration of the study period abroad. While the minority of those spending three or in a few cases less than three months (37 per cent) and of those spending four to six months abroad (42 per cent) continued to have considerable contact five years later, the respective proportion was higher than two-thirds for those who had spent abroad up to one year (68 per cent) or even more than one year (73 per cent).

Former ERASMUS students were additionally asked to specify the ways and extent to which they kept contact, being provided with a list of 10 respective items. As a factor analysis shows, the 10 aspects listed in the questionnaire represented three basic types of keeping contact: first, direct contacts to persons from the host country, second, collection of information regarding the host country, and third, participation in organized activities concerned with the host country. The proportion of graduates who stated frequent activities (1 or 2 on a scale from 1 = "very much" to 5 = "not at all") to the single items were as follows (see Table 6.9).

Regarding direct contact to persons from the host country,
- 57 per cent stated communication with persons living in the host country,
- 51 per cent kept in touch through travelling to the host country,
- 42 per cent received visitors from the host country, and
- 29 per cent had business contacts.

As regards collection of information regarding the host country,
- 53 per cent kept informed through reading or watching media,
- 36 per cent by reading popular journals/literature,
- 30 per cent by reading professional journals/literature, and
- 27 per cent by attending art exhibitions, concerts, cinema and other cultural activities.

As regards participation in organized activities,
- 11 per cent kept in touch by attending conferences, seminars, lectures etc. dealing with the host country, and
- 8 per cent by being members of organization(s) involved with the host country.

About three-quarters of former ERASMUS students travelled to the former host country within five years after the ERASMUS-supported period abroad. As purpose for their visits
- 40 per cent stated exclusively personal reasons,
- 9 per cent professional reasons only, and
- 29 per cent personal as well as professional reasons.

The number of visits were on average 3.3 in the case of professional visits and 4.1 in the case of personal visits. Respondents who stated professional visits spent for all visits on average 23.2 weeks in the host country. The total duration was 10 weeks on average per respondent for personal

Table 6.9

Ways of Maintaining Significant Contact with /Interest in the ERASMUS Host Country, by Host Country (per cent* of respondents five years after the ERASMUS-supported study period)

	Host country											Total
	B	D	DK	E	F	GR	I	IRL	NL	P	UK	
Reading or watching media on the host country	20	45	29	58	60	39	55	59	36	25	53	53
Communicating with persons living in the host country	44	68	14	72	61	33	62	35	52	50	50	57
Reading popular journals/literature from the host country	4	32	14	44	40	24	36	19	16	17	39	36
Reading professional journals/literature from the host country	12	35	14	33	31	18	22	16	16	8	35	30
Attending host country related conferences, seminars, lectures etc.	4	15	0	15	13	6	14	0	13	17	8	11
Being a member of organization(s) involved with the host country	0	13	0	8	8	0	16	3	11	0	5	8
Attending host country related art exhibitions, concerts, cinema etc.	17	16	0	36	31	12	31	32	16	8	27	27
Receiving visitors from the host country	36	52	14	61	42	17	48	27	43	42	35	42
Travelling to the host country	28	62	14	64	64	33	62	24	43	33	39	51
Through business contact	12	38	0	27	30	18	28	8	26	8	31	29

Questionnaire 3, question 6.2: How, and to what extent, have you maintained contact/interest in the country of your study period abroad since your return home?

* Categories 1 and 2 on a scale from 1 = "very much" to 5 = "not at all" visits. The proportion of respondents having spent the study period abroad in one of the small European countries who revisited their former host country in the following five years was below average, as was in most cases the number and duration of visits.

An analysis of the correlation between the decrease in knowledge and the extent of activities to keep contact with the host country shows significantly less loss of knowledge in the case of frequent contacts with host country people, reception of host country-related information or travelling to the host country.

Figure 6.3
Effort to Keep up Proficiency in Language of the Host Country of the ERASMUS-Supported Period Abroad by Host Country
(per cent of respondents five years after the ERASMUS study period)

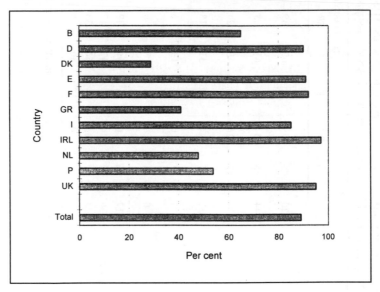

Questionnaire 3, question 6.4: Do you try to keep up your proficiency in the language of the host country in which you carried out your ERASMUS-supported study period?

Former ERASMUS students were also asked how they tried to keep up their proficiency in the language of the host country five years after the period abroad. Actually, 89 per cent of the former ERASMUS students who had spent the period in a country in which the dominant language was not their home country's language reported activities to keep up their linguistic proficiency. The respective quota was 92 per cent two years earlier, i.e. almost three years after the study period abroad.

Again, this proportion was relatively small among respondents who stayed in host countries with languages not widely known internationally. Less than half of respondents who stayed in Denmark, Greece and the Netherlands reported that they try to keep up their proficiency in language of the host country (see Figure 6.3).

As one might expect, books, newspapers, TV and other media were the most frequent tools for keeping up foreign language proficiency (70 per cent), followed by correspondence with persons from the host country (51 per cent). Thirteen per cent even took language courses.

The category "other" was chosen by almost 20 per cent of those naming measures of keeping up their foreign language proficiency. Most of them mentioned living in the host country as a means of keeping up the language proficiency (12 per cent).

Table 6.10
Means of Keeping up Proficiency in Language of the Host Country by Duration of the ERASMUS-Supported Study Period Abroad 1988/89
(per cent of respondents five years after the ERASMUS study period; multiple reply possible)

	Duration of study period abroad in months				Total
	3 or less	4 – 6	7 – 12	13 and more	
Language courses	18	14	11	4	13
Books, newspapers, radio, TV from that country	62	68	75	74	70
Correspondence with persons in that country	36	48	60	58	51
Other, namely	6	9	13	21	11
Living in the host country	11	9	12	19	12
Not ticked	25	19	11	6	16
Total	158	168	182	183	172
(n)	(266)	(418)	(455)	(89)	(1228)

Questionnaire 3, question 6.4: Do you try to keep up your proficiency in the language of the host country in which you carried out your ERASMUS-supported study period? If yes, please indicate by what means.

It is interesting to note that the shorter the study period was, the higher was the proportion of those taking courses in the host country language afterwards (see Table 6.10). It appears that there was a desire on the part of some of the students going abroad for a short period to learn more than was possible during such a short period. In contrast, correspondence with persons in the host country was more often reported the longer the period abroad lasted. Activities to keep up the foreign language proficiency, thus, seem to play in part a compensatory and in part a reinforcing role regarding the competences acquired prior to and during the study period abroad.

Chapter 7

Retrospective Assessment of Study Abroad

7.1 Assessment of Current Professional Situation

Almost three years after the ERASMUS-supported study period, a substantial proportion of former ERASMUS students had stated that study abroad was helpful for obtaining their first job and in being assigned the type of work tasks in which they were actually involved. However, the number of those stating a positive impact of the study period abroad on the level of their income was hardly higher than those stating a negative impact. We also noted that 24 per cent of graduates, when being surveyed almost three years after the study period abroad, considered themselves to be employed at too low a level in comparison to the educational qualification and degree. Thus, we could state that ERASMUS students have an edge in the search for employment and in getting work tasks related to international competences, but they are not rewarded in terms of superior positions.

Almost five years after the study period abroad, former ERASMUS students again were asked about their career opportunities. First, asked about their future chances of promotion (on a scale from 1 = "excellent" to 5 = "non-existent"),

- 52 per cent perceived high or excellent future chances of promotion,
- 25 per cent neither positive nor negative expectations, and
- 23 per cent very few or non-existent future chances of getting promoted in their current job.

After 31 months of job experience on average, more than half of former ERASMUS students were employed in organizations, institutions or companies which provided good or excellent possibilities for the future career. Graduates who presently see no chance for promotion in the future might change their employer to widen their opportunities or try working in areas where no established or foreseen career path exists (e.g. as teachers in primary or secondary school etc.). Highest proportion of former ERASMUS students who reported good or excellent future chances of promotion in their current job could be observed among those from Denmark (75 per cent, see Table 7.1). The respective proportions were also above average among former students from Belgium, Ireland (61 per cent each), the United Kingdom (58 per cent) and the Netherlands (57 per cent). Lowest future chances for promotion were reported by former students from Greece (44 per cent), Spain and France (46 per cent each). No noteworthy differences could be observed regarding the ERASMUS host country.

Table 7.1
Future Chances of Promotion in Job Held at the Time of the Third Survey, by Country of Home Institution of Higher Education
(per cent and mean of employed graduates responding five years after the ERASMUS-supported study period)

	Country of home institution											Total
	B	D	DK	E	F	GR	I	IRL	NL	P	UK	
1 = excellent	23	19	25	12	12	22	20	28	14	33	31	20
2	39	33	50	34	35	22	29	33	43	33	26	33
3	20	23	0	24	31	22	27	22	14	0	25	25
4	8	12	13	19	10	11	8	6	3	33	9	11
5 = non-existent	10	14	13	10	13	22	15	11	26	0	8	12
Total	100	100	100	100	100	100	100	100	100	100	100	100
(n)	(71)	(295)	(8)	(98)	(198)	(9)	(95)	(18)	(35)	(3)	(182)	(1012)
Mean	2.4	2.7	2.4	2.8	2.8	2.9	2.7	2.4	2.8	2.3	2.4	2.6

Questionnaire 3, question 4.12: In your current job, please estimate your future chances of promotion.

Former ERASMUS students in communication and information sciences (83 per cent), business studies (61 per cent), medical fields and mathematics (58 per cent each) and engineering (57 per cent) stated most often that they expected good future chances for promotion. The respective proportions were lowest in geography/geology (11 per cent), education and teacher training (18 per cent), art and design (25 per cent) and in foreign languages (36 per cent).

Table 7.2

Future Chances of Promotion in Job Held at the Time of the Third Survey, by Current Sector of Employment
(per cent and mean of employed graduates responding five years after the ERASMUS-supported study period)

	Agr	Ind	Com	Hig	Pri	Nat	Sem	Non	Int	Ser	Pro	Oth	Total
					Current employment sector*								
1 = excellent	20	22	27	14	4	14	14	5	14	24	25	18	20
2	40	38	37	28	17	31	41	25	7	33	33	18	33
3	0	23	23	26	30	29	24	40	43	20	28	18	25
4	20	9	5	14	25	7	7	15	21	15	5	18	11
5 = non-existent	20	9	9	18	23	19	14	15	14	9	9	29	13
Total	100	100	100	100	100	100	100	100	100	100	100	100	100
(n)	(5)	(255)	(175)	(130)	(69)	(72)	(29)	(20)	(14)	(136)	(81)	(17)	(1003)
Mean	2.8	2.5	2.3	3.0	3.4	2.9	2.7	3.1	3.1	2.5	2.4	3.2	2.6

Questionnaire 3, question 4.12: In your current job, please estimate your future chances of promotion.

* Explanation see Table 6.3

These figures have to be seen in their connection with the current sector of employment. As Table 7.2 shows, the private sector opens far better future chances for promotion than the public sector. Former ERASMUS students currently employed in commerce (63 per cent) or industry (60 per cent) reported most often good career opportunities. In the public and non-profit sectors the proportions of students who stated good future chances for promotion were below average. It was lowest among respondents employed in international, intergovernmental organizations (21 per cent), primary and secondary schools (22 per cent) and private non-profit organizations (30 per cent).

The duration of the ERASMUS-supported period abroad does not seem not to be of importance for the expectation of future career opportunities in current employment. There are slight differences, though, which seem to be spurious, because they turn out to be marginal, if controlled by economic sector.

Male respondents (61 per cent) harboured somewhat higher hopes for future promotion than female respondents (44 per cent). Even if we control the economic sector, some difference remains, though it seems to be smaller than popular arguments about gender differences regarding career opportunities suggest.

Former ERASMUS students were also asked almost five years after the study period abroad, as they had been asked two years previously, to state the appropriateness of their current occupation with respect to the level of position and the use of qualifications and skills in comparison to their educational qualification and degree (on a scale from 1 = "much too low" and 3 = "appropriate" to 5 = "much too high"). Both aspects turned out to be highly positively correlated (Pearson corr. of .6) which shows that a high position usually is connected with a high degree of utilization of qualifications and vice versa.

Altogether 28 per cent of former ERASMUS students considered their level of position as too low, 64 per cent as appropriate and 8 per cent as too high. The respective proportions were 24 per cent, 67 per cent and 9 per cent almost three years after the study period abroad. On average, former ERASMUS students perceived their status slightly more negatively in the most recent study.

As regards the use of qualifications and skills, the proportion of those stating too low was 33 per cent as compared with 59 per cent considering it appropriate and 8 per cent as too high. In comparison to the similar surveys on this topic available in various European countries, we might interpret this as normal or below the average of graduates from institutions of higher education. In any event the data confirm that former

ERASMUS students cannot expect to have above-average careers in general, but only a higher likelihood of access to tasks and assignments of tasks which require international experiences and skills.

Table 7.3
Appropriateness of Employment Held at the Time of the Third Survey as Regards Educational Qualification, by Country of Home Institution of Higher Education (per cent of employed graduates responding five years after the ERASMUS-supported study period)

	B	D	DK	E	F	GR	I	IRL	NL	P	UK	Total
					Country of home institution							Total
Level of position												
1 = much too low	4	7	0	7	9	17	7	17	8	0	9	8
2	7	19	0	21	24	33	31	22	18	0	22	21
3 = appropriate	81	67	75	58	61	33	57	61	61	67	65	64
4	8	7	25	15	6	17	5	0	13	33	4	8
5 = much too high	0	0	0	0	0	0	0	0	0	0	0	0
Total	100	100	100	100	100	100	100	100	100	100	100	100
Use of qualifications and skills												
1 = much too low	5	8	0	11	8	8	17	22	8	0	12	10
2	12	22	13	23	26	50	29	22	16	0	23	23
3 = appropriate	78	61	63	56	61	33	42	56	63	67	58	59
4	4	9	25	10	5	8	13	0	13	33	6	8
5 = much too high	0	0	0	1	0	0	0	0	0	0	1	0
Total	100	100	100	100	100	100	100	100	100	100	100	100
(n)	(73)	(297)	(8)	(102)	(209)	(12)	(96)	(18)	(38)	(3)	(183)	(1039)

Questionnaire 3, question 4.13: Comparing your educational qualification/degree with your current occupation (and the potential career opportunities which it offers), do you consider yourself as being employed at an appropriate level?

Too low positions as well as too low use of qualifications were most often reported by Greek (50 per cent and 58 per cent respectively), Irish (39 per cent and 44 per cent) and Italian graduates (38 per cent and 46 per cent). As Table 7.3 indicates, these three countries clearly stood out in this respect. The obvious problems of former ERASMUS students from these three countries in finding appropriate employment cannot be attributed to the composition according to fields of study. With the exception of Irish graduates these findings are similar to those of the survey conducted almost three years after the ERASMUS-supported period abroad.

A substantial proportion of graduates from social sciences (48 per cent) were in too low a position, from their point of view, as Table 7.4 shows. Low positions were even more often reported in communication sciences, agriculture, art and design and geography/geology, but the small absolute numbers should caution us: random effects cannot be excluded. On the other hand, some graduates from fields more likely to lead to expected positions also considered themselves as not employed at an appropriate level: 27 per cent of graduates from business studies, 23 per cent of graduates from medical fields, 16 per cent of engineering graduates and 13 per cent of law graduates. The use of qualifications and skills was considered as too low by about half of the graduates from agriculture, humanities, education/teacher training and communication sciences. Lowest proportions in this respect were reported by graduates from medical fields (8 per cent) and law (20 per cent).

Women (34 per cent) reported too low a position more frequently than men (23 per cent) as well as too low a use of qualifications and skills (36 per cent as compared to 29 per cent). If controlled by field of study, disadvantages of women with respect to the level of position could be observed most often in art and design, geography/geology, medical fields, natural sciences and communication sciences. On the other hand, more male than female graduates from social sciences, education/teacher training and agriculture reported too low a use of qualification in their current employment.

As Table 7.5 shows, the rating of appropriateness of position and use of qualification hardly varied by host country. This finding deserves attention. In contrast to the use of host country knowledge and the host country language, which were clearly linked to the size of the country and the frequency of international utilization of the language, this finding suggest that the choice of the host country only affects the utilization of very specific kinds of international knowledge, but not the utility of study abroad in general for a career.

A substantial number of graduates were dissatisfied with their income at the time the third survey was carried out. Asked about the appropriateness of their income as regards to the academic degree (on a scale from 1 = "considerably more than appropriate" to 5 = "considerably less than appropriate"),

- 43 per cent considered their income as less than appropriate;
- 45 per cent as appropriate and
- 12 per cent as higher than could be expected by the academic degree.

Table 7.4
Appropriateness of Employment Held at the Time of the Third Survey With Regard to Educational Qualification, by Field of Study During the ERASMUS-Supported Study Period Abroad 1988/89 (per cent of employed graduates responding five years after the ERASMUS study period)

	Agr	Arc	Art	Bus	Edu	Eng	Geo	Hum	Lan	Law	Mat	Med	Nat	Soc	Com	Other	Total
Level of position																	
1 = much too low	0	6	13	5	10	1	22	10	15	4	6	8	7	15	50	13	8
2	45	29	25	22	20	15	22	27	27	10	24	15	19	33	0	13	21
3 = appropriate	55	52	63	64	70	78	44	60	53	78	64	62	69	42	33	64	64
4	0	13	0	9	0	6	11	3	6	8	6	15	5	9	17	9	8
5 = much too high	0	0	0	0	0	0	0	0	0	1	0	0	0	0	0	0	0
Total	100	100	100	100	100	100	100	100	100	100	100	100	100	100	100	100	100
Use of qualifications and skills																	
1 = much too low	18	9	11	7	20	4	22	14	17	6	12	0	7	24	17	16	10
2	36	22	22	23	30	21	22	27	27	14	30	8	24	18	33	16	23
3 = appropriate	36	59	67	59	40	68	56	41	50	71	52	85	67	55	33	57	59
4	9	9	0	10	10	7	0	3	6	9	6	8	2	3	17	9	8
5 = much too high	0	0	0	0	0	0	0	0	1	0	0	0	0	0	0	2	0
Total	100	100	100	100	100	100	100	100	100	100	100	100	100	100	100	100	100
(n)	(11)	(32)	(9)	(375)	(10)	(114)	(9)	(29)	(168)	(111)	(33)	(13)	(42)	(33)	(6)	(44)	(1039)

Questionnaire 3, question 4.13: Comparing your educational qualification/degree with your current occupation (and the potential career opportunities which it offers), do you consider yourself as being employed at an appropriate level?

* Explanation see Table 3.8.

Table 7.5

**Appropriateness of Employment With Regard to Educational Quali-
fication, by Host Country** (per cent of employed graduates responding
five years after the ERASMUS-supported study period)

	B	D	DK	E	F	GR	I	IRL	NL	P	UK	Total
					Host country							Total
Level of position												
1 = much too low	8	10	0	10	7	0	10	12	10	0	6	8
2	17	23	20	27	22	22	17	6	22	29	20	21
3 = appropriate	58	62	80	53	65	61	63	68	65	71	66	64
4	17	5	0	9	6	17	10	15	2	0	8	8
5 = much too high	0	0	0	1	0	0	0	0	2	0	0	0
Total	100	100	100	100	100	100	100	100	100	100	100	100
**Use of qualifica-
tions and skills**												
1 = much too low	8	12	0	11	11	6	13	9	12	0	8	10
2	21	25	40	26	23	11	18	24	20	29	23	23
3 = appropriate	71	58	40	54	58	67	62	56	65	71	60	59
4	0	5	20	9	8	17	7	12	2	0	9	8
5 = much too high	0	0	0	0	1	0	0	0	2	0	0	0
Total	100	100	100	100	100	100	100	100	100	100	100	100
(n)	(24)	(130)	(5)	(91)	(279)	(18)	(60)	(34)	(51)	(7)	(340)	(1039)

Questionnaire 3, question 4.13: Comparing your educational qualification/degree with
your current occupation (and the potential career opportunities which it offers), do you
consider yourself as being employed at an appropriate level?

More than half of graduates from Greece (79 per cent), Ireland (59 per
cent) and Italy (53 per cent) rated their income as less than appropriate.
The assessment of the current income by graduates from the other countries did not differ very much from the average of all respondents. Only
the few Danish graduates stood clearly out in their positive rating of their
income, as Table 7.6 shows.

The lowest proportions of graduates who considered their income as
not appropriate in comparison to their academic degree could be observed
in business studies (32 per cent), mathematics and medical fields (33 per
cent each), natural sciences (34 per cent), engineering (37 per cent) and

law (41 per cent). Among graduates from all other fields, more than half considered their income as not appropriate. Women more often described their income as not appropriate to their academic degree than men (47 per cent as compared to 37 per cent). If controlled by field of study, a slight disadvantage for women as regards income remained.

Table 7.6

Appropriateness of Current Income at the Time of the Third Survey, by Country of Home Institution of Higher Education (per cent of employed graduates responding five years after the ERASMUS-supported study period)

	Country of home institution											Total
	B	D	DK	E	F	GR	I	IRL	NL	P	UK	
1 = considerably more than appropriate	3	2	14	0	0	7	0	0	0	0	2	1
2	5	13	43	10	9	0	7	12	11	0	12	10
3	58	49	14	46	45	14	40	29	49	67	43	45
4	27	23	29	30	34	43	23	41	19	33	30	28
5 = considerably less than appropriate	7	14	0	14	12	36	30	18	22	0	13	15
Total	100	100	100	100	100	100	100	100	100	100	100	100
(n)	(73)	(297)	(7)	(102)	(211)	(14)	(100)	(17)	(37)	(3)	(187)	(1048)

Questionnaire 3, question 4.14: To what extent do you think that your current income is appropriate to your academic degree?

Substantial proportions of graduates who were employed in the agriculture sector (78 per cent), primary or secondary schools (62 per cent), higher education (56 per cent) and private non-profit companies considered their income as not appropriate to their academic degree. The respective proportion was lowest in industry (28 per cent). The size of enterprises obviously played an important role in the level of income. Respondents employed in enterprises with more than 500 employees described their income significantly less often as not appropriate than graduates active in smaller enterprises (23 per cent as compared to 46 per cent).

About half of the graduates were satisfied with the professional situation at the time the survey was carried out (see Table 7.7). A further 28 per cent were neither satisfied nor dissatisfied, and 20 per cent were dissatisfied with their current employment.

Table 7.7
Overall Satisfaction with the Professional Situation, by Country of Home Institution of Higher Education (per cent and mean of employed graduates responding five years after the ERASMUS-supported study period)

	Country of home institution											Total
	B	D	DK	E	F	GR	I	IRL	NL	P	UK	
1 = very satisfied	32	19	50	14	24	7	12	6	33	0	14	19
2	42	36	13	37	26	29	32	29	20	100	32	33
3	18	27	25	31	28	21	23	53	28	0	33	28
4	5	14	13	12	16	29	26	12	15	0	14	15
5 = very dissatisfied	3	3	0	6	6	14	8	0	5	0	6	5
Total	100	100	100	100	100	100	100	100	100	100	100	100
(n)	(74)	(303)	(8)	(106)	(216)	(14)	(101)	(17)	(40)	(3)	(189)	(1071)
Mean	2.0	2.4	2.0	2.6	2.6	3.1	2.9	2.7	2.4	2.0	2.7	2.5

Questionnaire 3, question 4.15: How satisfied are you overall, regarding your professional situation?

Most satisfied were graduates from Belgium (73 per cent), Denmark (63 per cent) and Germany (56 per cent), whereas graduates from Ireland (35 per cent) and Greece (36 per cent) least often stated overall satisfaction with the professional situation. Regarding field of study, graduates from engineering (62 per cent), social sciences (59 per cent), business studies (58 per cent) and law (57 per cent) most often described the professional situation as satisfying. In contrast, among education and teacher training graduates only 8 per cent reported overall satisfaction in the current employment. Low were the respective proportions as well among graduates from art and design (28 per cent) and foreign languages (35 per cent).

Male graduates somewhat more often stated satisfaction with the professional situation than women (58 per cent as compared to 46 per cent). Again, this difference is smaller, if controlled by field of study. This finding matches those previously reported regarding future chances of promotion, level of position, use of qualifications and skills and current income.

A regression analysis shows that the overall satisfaction of graduates with the professional situation largely depends on the status they reached with respect to various aspects of status surveyed. The higher the income, the more future chances for promotion and the more appropriate the level of current occupation, the more satisfied were the graduates with their current professional situation in general.

7.2 Retrospective Assessment of Study Abroad

In retrospect, former ERASMUS students were asked to assess the value of study abroad according to various cultural, foreign language, academic and careers issues. Altogether, they considered the study abroad period supported by the ERASMUS programme as worthwhile. They rated 9 aspects addressed in the questionnaire on average 2.1 on a scale from 1 = "extremely worthwhile" to 5 = "not at all worthwhile".

In general, learning a foreign language and maturity and personal development were rated most positively (1.5 each). All aspects concerned with enhancement of knowledge and reflection such as knowledge about the host country, enhancement of academic and professional knowledge, new perspectives on the home country and new ways of thinking received intermediate ratings (between 1.7 and 2.1). As far as these items were also posed in the questionnaires shortly after and again three years after the ERASMUS-supported study period abroad, the ratings only changed slightly over the years.

The value of study abroad for the occupation as well as for career prospects was assessed five years after the study period abroad with some caution (2.5 each). Shortly after the period abroad and still almost three years later the expected value for career prospects was clearly higher (1.8 and 2.0 respectively).

As regards income, the former ERASMUS students rated the value of the study period abroad negatively on average (3.5). This item had not been included in the previous surveys.

Table 7.8 shows the different ratings according to host country. On average of the nine categories posed to former ERASMUS students, those who went to a larger country (Germany, France, United Kingdom, Italy and Spain) tend to consider their study abroad period more positively than those who spent their study period in a smaller country.

The same was true for the ratings shortly after return from the study period abroad as well as almost three years after the study period abroad.

This comparison, however, can be undertaken only with caution, because some of the items were differently phrased in the questionnaires.

Table 7.8

Personal Value of Study Abroad, by Host Country (mean* of respondents five years after the ERASMUS-supported study period)

	B	D	DK	E	F	GR	I	IRL	NL	P	UK	Total
					Host country							Total
Enhancement of academic and professional knowledge	2.2	2.0	2.1	2.1	2.1	2.5	2.1	2.2	2.0	2.3	2.2	2.1
Relevance to your job/occupation	2.8	2.4	3.3	2.6	2.5	3.2	2.4	2.4	2.9	2.9	2.3	2.5
Income/salary	3.9	3.3	4.4	3.7	3.5	3.9	3.5	3.8	4.0	4.4	3.4	3.5
Career prospects	3.2	2.3	3.4	2.6	2.5	3.1	2.5	2.7	3.3	3.2	2.3	2.5
Foreign language proficiency	2.5	1.4	2.4	1.5	1.4	2.4	1.6	1.3	3.0	3.0	1.4	1.5
New perspectives on home country	2.4	2.0	1.6	2.0	2.1	2.5	2.0	1.8	2.2	2.6	1.9	2.0
New ways of thinking and reflection	2.4	1.9	1.9	1.9	2.0	2.5	2.0	1.9	2.0	2.6	1.9	2.0
Knowledge and understanding of the host country	1.8	1.6	2.1	1.5	1.6	2.3	1.7	1.8	2.1	2.1	1.7	1.7
Maturity and personal development	1.6	1.5	1.4	1.3	1.5	1.8	1.6	1.4	1.6	1.8	1.4	1.5
(n)	(25)	(146)	(7)	(111)	(324)	(19)	(80)	(38)	(57)	(12)	(406)	(1225)

Questionnaire 3, question 7.1: From your point of view today, to what extent do you consider your study abroad worthwhile with regard to the following?

* On a scale from 1 = "extremely worthwhile" to 5 = "not at all worthwhile"

The longer the duration of the study period abroad, the more highly its value was appreciated (see Table 7.9). Between those spending at most three months abroad and those spending more than one year abroad the ratings differ substantially (.8 on average). Highest differences could be observed regarding the value of the period abroad for the level of income, career prospects and relevance for the occupation.

As already stated, shortly after return from the study period abroad as well as almost three years later, the few ERASMUS students from geography/geology and communication and information sciences valued the study period less highly than those from other fields. This was even more pronounced five years later (2.8 and 2.7 respectively) than shortly after the return (2.2 each) and almost three years after return (2.6 and 2.4 respectively). On the other hand, former students of foreign languages, business studies and engineering rated the ERASMUS-supported study period most positively.

Table 7.9

Personal Value of Study Abroad, by Duration of the ERASMUS-Supported Study Period Abroad 1988/89 (mean* of respondents five years after the ERASMUS study period)

	Duration of study period abroad in months				Total
	3 or less	4 – 6	7 – 12	13 and more	
Enhancement of academic and professional knowledge	2.3	2.2	1.9	1.7	2.1
Relevance to your job/ occupation	2.9	2.6	2.3	1.9	2.5
Income/salary	3.9	3.7	3.3	2.6	3.5
Career prospects	3.0	2.6	2.2	1.7	2.5
Foreign language proficiency	2.0	1.5	1.3	1.2	1.5
New perspectives on your home country	2.3	2.0	1.8	1.7	2.0
New ways of thinking and reflection	2.3	2.0	1.9	1.6	2.0
Knowledge and understanding of the host country	1.9	1.7	1.6	1.4	1.7
Maturity and personal development	1.6	1.5	1.4	1.3	1.5

Questionnaire 3, question 7.1: From your point of view today, to what extent do you consider your study abroad worthwhile for with regard to the following?

* On a scale from 1 = "extremely worthwhile" to 5 = "not at all worthwhile"

7.3 General Satisfaction

Asked five years later to rate their satisfaction with their study period abroad ("all things considered") on a scale from 1 = "very satisfied" to 5 = "not satisfied at all", former ERASMUS students rated 1.4 on average. This figure is slightly better than the average rating shortly after return from the study period abroad and almost three years later (1.5 each).

Actually, 94 per cent of those responding to the third questionnaire were satisfied (ratings of 1 or 2).

The best ratings five years later were given by former students from Greece (1.2), Spain, France and Portugal (1.3 each). Irish students were slightly less satisfied (1.7).

As regards host country, we note that satisfaction with a study period in Portugal was slightly less positive in retrospect than satisfaction with a study period in other European countries (see Table 7.10). Otherwise differences were small.

Table 7.10

Satisfaction with Study Period Abroad in Retrospect, by Host Country (per cent and mean* of all respondents five years after the ERASMUS-supported study period)

	Host country											Total
	B	D	DK	E	F	GR	I	IRL	NL	P	UK	
1 = very satisfied	63	77	57	73	67	53	64	76	62	33	71	69
2	38	16	43	18	26	47	26	24	31	42	24	25
3	0	6	0	7	6	0	10	0	7	25	4	5
4	0	1	0	2	1	0	0	0	0	0	0	1
5 = very dissatisfied	0	0	0	0	0	0	0	0	0	0	0	0
Total	100	100	100	100	100	100	100	100	100	100	100	100
(n)	(24)	(146)	(7)	(110)	(327)	(19)	(80)	(38)	(58)	(12)	(406)	(1227)
Mean	1.4	1.3	1.4	1.4	1.4	1.5	1.5	1.2	1.4	1.9	1.3	1.4

Questionnaire 3, question 7.2: In retrospect and all things considered, how satisfied are you with your study period abroad?

* On a scale from 1 = "very satisfied" to 5 = "very dissatisfied"

Chapter 8

Summary of Major Findings

Study for some period in another European country is aimed to broaden academic experience, to contribute to personal development by means of acquiring new cultural experience, and also, in most cases, to improve foreign language proficiency. Last but not least, many students partici- pating in the ERASMUS programme hope that competencies acquired during the study period abroad will later prove useful in the graduates' career.

This study reports the major findings of a survey of former ERASMUS students undertaken about five years after the ERASMUS-supported study period abroad. 1,234 persons having been awarded an ERASMUS grant during the academic year 1988/89, the second year of the ERAS- MUS programme, responded to the short written questionnaire mailed to them in spring 1994.

The same persons had already reported their experiences in winter 1989/90, shortly after the ERASMUS-supported study period, as well as in spring 1992, i.e. almost three years after the study period abroad. This longitudinal setting of the study allows us to examine, among other things, whether those rating their studies as academically successful upon return perceive a better utilization of the study experiences abroad upon graduation, whether estimates regarding the prolongation of the overall study period due to the study period abroad turn out to be valid, or how retrospective assessment of the study period abroad changes over time.

Of the respondents to the third questionnaire, 34 per cent had spent 4 – 6 months and 37 per cent 7 – 12 months abroad with the support of the ERASMUS programme in 1988/89. Twenty-two per cent had spent three months or in a few cases a shorter period, whereas 7 per cent stayed even more than one year in the host country.

At the time of the second survey, i.e. almost three years after the study period abroad, more than three-quarters of the former ERASMUS stu- dents had graduated. Five years after the study period abroad, eventually 94 per cent of the respondents report that they graduated.

According to the former ERASMUS students' estimates five years after the study period in another European country, their overall study period was prolonged by 2.9 months due to the study period abroad. This was slightly less than expected initially (i.e. shortly after the study period abroad), but still about 40 per cent of the study period abroad.

Former ERASMUS students turned out to be very education and training-minded. Fifty-three per cent took up further study or training between graduation and the time the third survey was conducted.

At the time the third survey was conducted, 86 per cent of those former ERASMUS students who had been awarded a degree actually are employed – 79 per cent full-time and 7 per cent part-time. Five per cent name education and training as their major activity, 4 per cent report that they are unemployed, and 5 per cent state other activities.

Only about one-third of former ERASMUS students are employed in the public sector. More than half report assignment in industry, commerce and other private service. Nine per cent are self-employed or employed in areas dominated by self-employed professionals.

ERASMUS studies obviously help mobility. About a third of former ERASMUS students reports that they were offered employment abroad. Of those former ERASMUS students employed at the time of the third survey, 19 per cent are actually employed abroad, among them almost half in the ERASMUS host country.

Criteria related to the international dimension were not among the most important for former ERASMUS students when seeking employment. However, 59 per cent state the application of foreign language skills and 39 per cent the opportunity of working in a foreign country as one of their major criteria when seeking employment. Asked about the criteria their employers had in mind in hiring them, 64 per cent of former ERASMUS perceive foreign language proficiency, 53 per cent the study period abroad, and 15 per cent the reputation of the host institution of higher education as one of the major criteria, viewed as the second, fourth and tenth most important on a list of 13 items provided in the respective question.

Most former ERASMUS students are employed in organizations which have continuous contacts with other countries, about half of which are with the respondents' respective ERASMUS host countries. The frequent link between study experience abroad and subsequent job assignment is certainly underscored by the fact that about half of the former ERASMUS students continuously make use on the job of the host country language and 30 per cent of first hand professional knowledge of the host country. There are about one-fifth of the respondents, though, who do not observe any direct professional utilization at all of those competences acquired or reinforced during the study period abroad.

The majority of former ERASMUS students consider themselves well qualified in the host country language and also believe that have acquired a substantial knowledge of the host country. As one might expect, ratings of these proficiencies were slightly lower five years later than they had been immediately after or about three years after the ERASMUS-supported study period in other European countries. Most respondents emphasize, however, that they choose various means of keeping up their respective competences.

Many former ERASMUS students are convinced that temporary study in another European country in the framework of the ERASMUS programme has helped in obtaining employment and was instrumental in access to work assignments which require international knowledge and experience. Also, the unemployment ratio of 4 per cent can be considered as relatively low.

In contrast to high-flying hopes sometimes publicly expressed, however, former ERASMUS students do not seem to have above-average early professional careers. About five years later, 28 per cent consider their position inappropriate in comparison to their degree, and 33 per cent state too low a utilization of their skills. On average, former ERASMUS students do not perceive any positive impact of the study period abroad on their income.

After almost five years, former ERASMUS students consider the study period almost as worthwhile as they rated it shortly after return. "All things considered", they seem to be even slightly more satisfied than they were shortly after return. However, they rate the value of study abroad for their occupation and career clearly more cautiously than they did before: the respective average ratings regarding career prospects dropped from 1.8 to 2.0 to eventually 2.5 on a five-point scale from "extremely worthwhile" to "not at all worthwhile".

The duration of the ERASMUS-supported study period abroad turned out to have a substantial impact. It is very instrumental for the utilization of study experience abroad after graduation, for future foreign language learning and contacts with the host country as well as for the assessment of the value of study abroad by former ERASMUS students. Study abroad of only three months consistently and up to at most half a year in many respects seems to have a much lesser impact of this kind than study abroad for longer periods.

As regards fields of study, obviously different factors come into play. Former students of foreign language studies, business studies and engineering students rate the ERASMUS-supported period abroad most positively – i.e. former students of most fields which are strongly represented in the ERASMUS programmes. As regards career, status and income and the respective impacts of study, graduates in business studies, law, medical fields, engineering, mathematics and natural sciences are more satisfied than graduates from other fields – this obviously reflects general differences of employment prospects according to field of study more strongly than specific impacts of study abroad. Finally, graduates from foreign languages, business studies and education/teacher training perceive the highest direct utilization of competences acquired or reinforced during the study period abroad – knowledge of the host countries and foreign language proficiency is most directly applied in professional fields related to the respective disciplines. Across these different dimensions, graduates from business studies are consistently among those gaining strongly from study abroad. It should be noted, though, that satisfaction with the study period abroad varies only to a limited extent according to the field of study.

Women describe their career, the impact of study on their careers and also the extent of the professional utilization of their knowledge related to study abroad experience somewhat less positively than men. If controlled by field of study, the respective differences are clearly smaller than one might expect on the basis of popular debate on gender differences of graduate careers.

Regarding the home country of the respondents, differences are by and large less marked than according to host country. As far as differences are noteworthy, various factors come into play as well. Former Greek, Irish and Italian ERASMUS students report least satisfactory careers – a finding which certainly reflects the general labour market. British and Irish respondents most often state that their employers cared little about foreign languages and study experiences abroad in hiring them – the importance of English as an international language seems to tempt British and Irish employers more often than others not to regard international competences highly. Finally, as regards the general appreciation of the value of study abroad, Southern European students and graduates are inclined to most positive ratings: this seems to reflect primarily a widely believed gradual quality difference of higher education which makes it more worthwhile to study abroad in the north.

Conversely, perceived quality differences and conditions of the national labour market come into play as well in differences of careers, the impact of study abroad on career and also the extent of utilization of competences acquired or reinforced during the study period. Beyond that, we note that the highest proportions of persons who spent their study period in Germany, Italy and France were eventually employed in the host country of their ERASMUS study period abroad. The strongest host country impact, however, is that of the size of the host country. This became clearly more visible five years after graduation than it had been in the earlier surveys of this longitudinal study. Persons who had spent their ERASMUS-supported period 1988/89 in one of the smaller countries of the European Community (including the Netherlands) clearly work less often in organizations having continuous contacts with the host country, have clearly less opportunity of using professionally the competences they acquired or increased during the study period abroad and clearly consider study abroad less directly useful for their assignments. As one might expect, foreign language learning in Ireland turned out to be the only exception in these respects.

As the ratings of the appropriateness of the position and of the use of qualification vary only to a limited extent, we might infer that study abroad also has general impacts on the career which are valuable across the various host countries. If it comes to the professional use of specific country-related and foreign language competences, however, the value of studying abroad in various European countries is unevenly distributed.

Altogether, experiences within five years after the ERASMUS-supported period suggest that ERASMUS study is not the gate to advanced careers. Also, about a fifth of former graduates do not note any direct value of the competences acquired abroad for their work assignment. Though some hopes were not fulfilled and some assessments became more cautious over time, former ERASMUS students retrospectively rate the value of study abroad very highly. This is not only due to the general appreciation of the cultural value of this experience. Rather, most of former ERASMUS students note considerable professional opportunities to use the competences the study period abroad fosters, and ERASMUS experiences obviously are a valuable asset for international careers.

ERASMUS Monographs

1. **Student Mobility within ERASMUS 1987/88 – A Statistical Survey**

   U. Teichler, F. Maiworm, W. Steube
   Arbeitspapiere, 24, Wissenschaftliches Zentrum für Berufs- und Hochschulforschung, Kassel 1990
   Contact: Prof. Ulrich TEICHLER, Wissenschaftliches Zentrum für Berufs- und Hochschulforschung, Universität GH Kassel, Henschelstraße 4, D-34109 Kassel; Tel.: 49-561-804 2415, Fax: 49-561-804 3301

2. **L'amélioration de la préparation linguistique et socioculturelle des étudiants ERASMUS**

   G. Baumgratz-Gangl, N. Deyson, G. Kloss
   Unité langues pour la Coopération en Europe (ULCE) auprès du Centre d'Information et de Recherche sur l'Allemagne Contemporaine (CIRAC), July 1989
   Contact: SOCRATES and Youth, rue Montoyer 70, B-1040 Bruxelles; Tel. 32-2-233 01 11, Fax: 32-2-2330150

3. **Recognition: A Typological Overview of Recognition Issues Arising in Temporary Study Abroad**

   U. Teichler
   Werkstattberichte, 29, Wissenschaftliches Zentrum für Berufs- und Hochschulforschung, Kassel 1990
   Contact: cf. Monograph No. 1

4. **Untersuchung über die Beteiligung der Medizin im ERASMUS-Programm (Study on the Participation of Medicine in ERASMUS)**

   In German with an English summary
   K. Schnitzer, E. Kort
   HIS Hochschulplanung 85, HIS (Hochschul-Informations-System GmbH), Hannover 1990
   Contact: Dr. Klaus SCHNITZER, HIS Hochschul-Informations-System, Postfach 2920, D-3000 Hannover; Tel.: 49-511-1220297, Fax: 49-511-1220250

5. **Teacher Education and the ERASMUS Programme**

    M. Bruce

    In: *European Journal of Teacher Education*, Vol. 12, No. 3, 1989 (pp.197 – 228) ISSN 0261-9768

    Contact: A.T.E.E. – Association for Teacher Education in Europe, rue de la Concorde 51, B-1050 Bruxelles; Tel.: 32-2-512 1734, Fax: 32-2-512 3265

6. **Les obstacles à la participation au programme ERASMUS dans le domaine de l'art et du design**

    P. Kuentz

    Strasbourg, July 1989

    Contact: Prof. Pierre KUENTZ, Ecole des Arts Decoratifs, 1 rue de l'Académie, F-6700 Strasbourg; Tel.: 33-88-353858

7. **ERASMUS et les arts du spectacle (musique, théâtre, danse)**

    D. Barriolade

    EUROCREATION, Paris, July 1989

    Contact: Denise Barriolade, EUROCREATION, L'agence française des jeunes créateurs européens, 3 rue Debelleyme, F-75003 Paris; Tel.: 33-1-48047879, Fax: 33-1-40299246

8. **Comparative Evaluation of ERASMUS ICPs in the Subject Areas of Business Management, Chemistry, History**

    Prof. A. Monasta

    Università di Firenze, July 1989

    Contact: Prof. Attilio MONASTA, Università degli Studi di Firenze, Facoltà di Magistero, Dipartemento di Scienze dell' Educazione, Via Cavour, 82, I-50129 Firenze; Tel.: 39-55-2757751/2757761

9. **Survey of Academic Recognition within the Framework of ICPs in the Field of Mechanical Engineering**

    H. Risvig Henriksen

    SEFI (Société Européenne pour la Formation des Ingénieurs), Bruxelles, August 1989

    Contact: SEFI, rue de la Concorde 51, B-1050 Bruxelles; Tel.: 32-2-512 1734, Fax: 32-2-512 3265

10. **ERASMUS PROGRAMME – Report on the Experience Acquired in the Application of the ERASMUS Programme 1987 – 1989**
    Commission of the European Communities, SEC(89) 2051, Brussels, December 1989
    Contact: cf. Monograph No. 2

11. **La coopération inter-universitaire dans les sciences agrono miques, ERASMUS 1978/88 – 1990/91**
    Philippe Ruffio
    ENSAR, Département des Sciences économiques et sociales, June 1990
    Contact: cf. Monograph No. 2

12. **Student Mobility 1988/89 - A Statistical Profile**
    U. Teichler, R. Kreitz, F. Maiworm
    Arbeitspapiere, 26, Wissenschaftliches Zentrum für Berufs- und Hochschulforschung, Kassel 1991
    Contact: cf. Monograph No. 1

13. **Experiences of ERASMUS Students 1988/89**
    U. Teichler
    Werkstattberichte, 32, Wissenschaftliches Zentrum für Berufs- und Hochschulforschung, Kassel 1991
    Contact: cf. Monograph No. 1

14. **Learning in Europe: The ERASMUS Experience**
    F. Maiworm, W. Steube, U. Teichler
    Jessica Kingsley Publishers, London 1991
    Contact: Jessica Kingsley Publishers, 118 Pentonville Road, UK-London N1 9JN; Tel.: 44-71833 2307, Fax 44-71-837 2917

15. **ECTS in its Year of Inauguration: The View of the Students**
    F. Maiworm, W. Steube, U. Teichler
    Werkstattberichte, 37, Wissenschaftliches Zentrum für Berufs- und Hochschulforschung, Kassel 1992
    Contact: cf. Monograph No. 1

15b. ECTS dans l'année de son lancement: le regard des étudiants

F. Maiworm, W. Steube, U. Teichler
Werkstattberichte, 39, Wissenschaftliches Zentrum für Berufs- und
Hochschulforschung, Kassel 1992
Contact: cf. Monograph No. 1

**16. ERASMUS Student Mobility Programmes 1989/90 in the View
of Their Coordinators.** Select Findings of the ICP Coordinators'
Reports.

F. Maiworm, W. Steube, U. Teichler
Werkstattberichte, 41, Wissenschaftliches Zentrum für Berufs- und
Hochschulforschung, Kassel 1993
Contact: cf. Monograph No. 1

**16a. Les programmes ERASMUS en matière de mobilité des
étudiants au cours de l'année 1989/90.** Analyse présentée à partir
des points de vue des coordinateurs.

F. Maiworm, W. Steube, U. Teichler
Werkstattberichte, 41a, Wissenschaftliches Zentrum für Berufs- und
Hochschulforschung, Kassel 1993
Contact: cf. Monograph No.1

17. Experiences of ERASMUS Students 1990/91

F. Maiworm, W. Steube, U. Teichler
Werkstattberichte, 42, Wissenschaftliches Zentrum für Berufs- und
Hochschulforschung, Kassel 1993
Contact: cf. Monograph No. 1

17a. Les expériences des étudiants ERASMUS en 1990/91

F. Maiworm, W. Steube, U. Teichler
Werkstattberichte, 42a, Wissenschaftliches Zentrum für Berufs- und
Hochschulforschung, Kassel 1993
Contact: cf. Monograph No. 1

**18. Transition to Work: The Experiences of Former ERASMUS
Students**

U. Teichler, F. Maiworm
Jessica Kingsley Publishers, London 1993
Contact: cf. Monograph No. 14

19. **ERASMUS Student Mobility Programmes 1991/92 in the View of the Local Directors**

    F. Maiworm and U. Teichler
    Werkstattberichte, 46, Wissenschaftliches Zentrum für Berufs- und Hochschulforschung, Kassel 1995
    Contact: cf. Monograph No. 1

20. **The First Years of ECTS in the View of the Students**

    F. Maiworm and U. Teichler
    Werkstattberichte, 47, Wissenschaftliches Zentrum für Berufs- und Hochschulforschung, Kassel 1995
    Contact: cf. Monograph No. 1

21. **Study Abroad and Early Career: Experiences of Former ERASMUS Students**

    F. Maiworm and U. Teichler
    Jessica Kingsley Publishers, London 1996
    Contact: cf. Monograph No. 14

22. **The Context of ERASMUS: A Survey of Institutional Management and Infrastructure in Support of Mobility and Co-operation**

    F. Maiworm, W. Sosa and U. Teichler
    Werkstattberichte, 49, Wissenschaftliches Zentrum für Berufs- und Hochschulforschung, Kassel 1996
    Contact: cf. Monograph No. 1